DRIVEN

How to Elevate Your Success as an
Entrepreneur

Adam Torres and Elliot Kallen

Mr. Century City, LLC

Beverly Hills, CA 90212
www.MissionMatters.com

Paperback ISBN: 978-1-949680-61-4

Ebook ISBN: 978-1-949680-60-7

DRIVEN

CONTENTS

Introduction   1

Part One

A Tale of Two Entrepreneurs

  1. The Accidental Entrepreneur   7
      – Adam Torres

  2. The Serial Entrepreneur   15
      – Elliot Kallen

  3. Meeting in the Metaverse   23
      – Adam Torres

Part Two

Mission-Based Entrepreneurship

  4. Without Vision, Nothing Happens   31
      – Elliot Kallen

  5. Just Get Started   39
      – Adam Torres

  6. Blows to the Side of the Head   53
      – Elliot Kallen

  7. Community Doesn't Just Happen   65
      – Elliot Kallen

8. Character Counts   69
– Elliot Kallen

9. Your Story Matters   81
– Adam Torres

10. Deal with What Is   91
– Elliot Kallen

11. Leadership is Not Glamorous   101
– Elliot Kallen

12. Balance is an Illusion   111
– Elliot Kallen

Part Three
You Can Do It

13. Your Brand Matters   121
– Adam Torres

14. Confidence is Half the Battle   133
– Elliot Kallen

15. Impact Your World   139
– Elliot Kallen

Conclusion   145

An Invitation from Adam Torres   147

An Invitation from Elliot Kallen   149

Appendix   150
About A Brighter Day Charity
  Core Programs
  Ways to Support
  Get in Touch
  Recommended Reading

INTRODUCTION

We wrote this book for the dreamers of entrepreneurial success, for current and future leaders, and to humanize the entrepreneurial experience. The entrepreneurial journey is far from a straight line to success. This journey is fraught with challenges and obstacles. We want you to understand the importance of never losing your vision, and the key to success is tenacity and perseverance. There is no failure unless you quit. There are only learning lessons that are a natural part of the process.

The media focuses on entrepreneurial wunderkinds like Elon Musk and Bill Gates. That can create a pressure, which causes us to think we need to have it all figured out, and we have to get it right the first time. The goal of this book is to show you some of the challenges and roadblocks we experienced, and to let you know you are not alone. You are in good company. Entrepreneurship is not supposed to be easy. If it was, everyone would be doing it.

This book will resonate with new leaders and entrepreneurs, as well as people who are well along their journey of starting, failing, succeeding and selling companies, as well as succeeding in the world of corporate leadership. People starting out want to know there's a track for them and that it's not based on whether they came out of a poor urban setting or a wealthy white-collar setting. It's about what you have inside you. It's about having the character and tenacity to develop a vision and see it through.

When you decide to be an entrepreneur, it usually doesn't fit what other people think you should be doing. People may say you're crazy. It's not that people around you don't care about you or don't want to support you. They just don't understand your dream. If you have a dream, we want to encourage you to go after it, because you'll never know if you don't try.

There is no single definition of success. Society says you define success by the size of your bank account. And, yes, that is absolutely a measure of success. Your balance sheet and bank account are signs of wealth. But success can be measured in ways other than wealth. Your goal may be to positively touch a million people with your product or your story. That's the difference between being wealthy and being rich.

Wealth is all about the things you can grab right now: a nice suit, a fast car, a beautiful home. Those are all wonderful things to have. However, being rich is about what you have inside. It's about the depth of your friendships, the love of your family and the joy your success creates. That's a better way to measure success. When life is coming to an end, no one wishes they had worked more or made more money. You will be judged by the depth of your character and how you touched the people around you. Living a rich life should be an even greater driver of motivation than being wealthy. That's not to minimize being wealthy, because we do have to live in the material world, and wealth brings both blessings and opportunities. But success is a long game.

Success is both a journey and an evolution. The youthful desires for things like a bright red Ferrari, mature into a desire to provide jobs and opportunities for others. We celebrate the successes of people in our communities, and it's exciting to see how our definitions of success continue to evolve through the years.

Our wildest dream is that this book will become a companion to your journey through entrepreneurship or your executive work life. The stories in this book are timeless ones that you can reflect on and revisit time and time again. As you read and reread this book at different stages of your life, the stories will take on new and different meanings and will resonate in different ways.

We hope this book becomes a friend along your path of entrepreneurship. We hope it helps you find your own personal vision that doesn't need to be approved by everyone, and that it helps you put a game plan together to achieve your vision. Once you have a clear vision and a solid plan, just remember to be flexible and adjust your course as you go. And remember above all else to never give up. Your character, strength and fortitude will carry you. There's no reason to sell your soul along the way to success. Ultimately, you will be judged, not merely on your accomplishments, but also on who you are along the way.

—Adam Torres and Elliot Kallen

PART ONE

A TALE OF TWO ENTREPRENEURS

MR. CENTURY CITY, LLC

Chapter One

The Accidental Entrepreneur

– Adam Torres

"Success is never accidental."

~ Jack Dorsey

G rowing up, I was an airbrush artist, and I spent hours and hours in the studio. When I wasn't playing basketball with my friends, I was making art. By the time I was in the seventh grade, I was already selling airbrushed T-shirts, which was a trend back then. Many of the kids at school were wearing my airbrushed shirts, and I made quite a bit of money doing that... until the day a teacher found me with a pocket full of money, and asked me what was going on. I assured her I was only selling shirts. Looking back, I didn't realize I was only a kid. In my mind, I was an adult with a business selling shirts. That was my first accidental experience with business.

Another experience that shaped my early concepts of business was when I found myself in a meeting with my parents, listening to a person who wanted to sign them up for Amway. My parents looked at me, and said, "We don't want to do this, but do you want to?" I said, "Sure, I'll sell some cleaning products." I started selling Amway under my parents' names. That's when I decided selling was kind of fun. You give people stuff, they're happy, and you make some money.

Having a love for art, but also a knack for business, made picking what I wanted to do when I grew up difficult.

My high school, Cass Technical High School, was a college preparatory school, which was unique in Detroit, when most public school kids at the time were not necessarily expected to go to college. The school wanted me to pick a major, like you do in college. I remember being in the counselor's office, trying to decide if I wanted to go into business or art. They were two very different curriculums. Making a decision like that as an eighth grader going into high school was just as life changing as when an 18-year-old picks a major when entering college.

I eventually chose business, because all the advice I was getting from my network suggested I couldn't make money as an artist. Now, looking at all the platforms that exist today, I could have made a lot of money in the art and design field. But I guess that wasn't my path.

Today, I give quite a few speeches to high schools and colleges, and I find myself reflecting back to my school days and how I can impact these children in a positive way. I always tell students that they have to watch who they're getting their advice from. Sometimes I ask students if any of them want to be a doctor? Then I ask, who gave them advice on how to become a doctor? A lot of them say their mom or dad. When I ask if their mom or dad is a doctor, they usually say no.

I inform them that may not be the best advice, because they don't know what it means to be a doctor. I also express that it is important to get advice from people who have actually done what you want to do. Then they will know if they are on the right path, or wasting valuable years heading in the wrong direction.

When I was their age, my parents didn't give me advice on things they didn't know, which was a luxury for me growing up. My mom was a social worker and my dad painted cars. Luckily, my parents were smart enough to know they were not the ones to give me financial or business advice. Instead, they found people who were successful in business, and introduced them into my life, so I could ask them questions.

During my junior and senior years of high school, I attended school for two or three hours a day, then I went to work at a brokerage firm. It was a kind of internship, where I received credits for the hours I worked. Of course, I was unlicensed, due to my age, so I worked in the back office of the IRA department at Raymond James and Associates, Inc., which was then located at 1 Griswold Street, across from the iconic Hart Plaza, in Downtown Detroit.

I went on to study international relations at the James Madison College, at Michigan State University. After graduation, I became an intern in the executive office of the Michigan Attorney General at the time, Mike Cox, thanks to the guidance of our good family friend, Mike Garavaglia, who is a successful businessman and mentor. I then worked for a lobbyist.

I was accepted into law school, and thought that was a good path, because I wanted to go into politics full time. Since I had a year before law school started, I joined my buddy, Adam Hengesbaugh, working at a mortgage company, called Rock Financial. I thought it would be a short gig, until I discovered I was pretty decent at sales. I was number one out of all the brokers who had been with the company for less than two years.

I literally used to sleep at the office, so I could pick up the phone at night. I helped people sign mortgage documents at three or four in the morning when they got off work. I was killing it. After about three months, they announced a restructuring, and moved us all to Quicken Loans. While this move was great for the majority of the people at the company, it did not suit me, so I took it as a sign for a change.

At the time, I had a girlfriend in Arizona, who was my college sweetheart, and I had been flying back and forth to see her. Once the job at Quicken Loans changed, it was a no-brainer to move to Phoenix, where I found a job selling insurance. This was hardcore sales, calling people, knocking on doors, sitting in living rooms, where you made sure to get the check before you leave the home kind of sales. If there was one lesson in all of that, it would be that I learned the value of systems and processes.

The company, American Income Life, was outstanding. It basically had two insurance instruments, which they turned into a very large supplemental life insurance business. And they did it through systems and processes with salespeople. They had scripts the salespeople had to memorize and we would videotape ourselves giving mock presentations. We were like actors, honing our tone of voice and facial expressions. The company and the employees were well-oiled and well-tuned machines.

I remember having a bad week once. I just wasn't selling. The management told me to go into the conference room and tape myself giving a mock presentation to an imaginary husband and wife. The tape immediately showed my problem. I learned that every single word you say matters. I was talking to the husband, and leaving out the wife. During my next real presentation, I corrected that and closed the deal. That's how the company improved my sales techniques, they were that good. They had it down to a science.

The company had a good product and the rates were fine, but it had incredible revenue, without doing any fancy marketing. Instead, the company focused on its salespeople, process and execution. It was a 60-year-old company, still using an old school postcard lead system, where a prospect mails in a postcard for more information, and is then followed up with by a salesperson. I learned that if you have the right processes, even old school can work. Due to what I learned at that job, the power of systems and processes still interests me today.

I eventually decided to leave the insurance business, because I didn't want to talk about dying anymore. In the beginning, it didn't bother me. I was making good money. But every single night I was in someone's home, at their kitchen table, talking about death. I know firefighters and police get the credit for protecting people, but life insurance salespeople also get credit in my opinion. The sales process takes a lot out of you mentally and emotionally to protect families. You're talking about a product that benefits the family members of the person who buys it. And whenever you bring up the topic, they want to tell you about when one of their loved ones died and include everything that happened. It's always their worst story. Life insurance salespeople have to talk about death all day long. For me, it was emotionally exhausting after time, and I knew I was ready to move on.

While looking for what other jobs I could do within the financial services business, I found Vanguard. I started working in the small business department, doing retirement plans for small business owners. I could have gone the asset management route and worked behind the scenes, but I preferred helping small business owners directly—who are still my clients today.

What attracted me to Vanguard was the opportunity to get my licenses. Also, I got to work indoors. I wasn't driving around to see people in their homes. It was a good job with a great culture and environment. If Vanguard taught me anything, it would be the importance of culture. The company culture at Vanguard is so strong, its clients are deeply loyal. And so are its employees.

Vanguard had a culture, from the top down, of watching every penny. When I was there, there were no paper cups at Vanguard. You had to bring your own coffee cup. The executive staff all flew commercial seating at the time. It is a company that has seven trillion in global assets under its management. It is known as the highest value, low cost provider, and for good reason. The company looks at basis points, because every basis point it saves, means more money that goes into its investors' pockets. Even internally, the leaders of the company walk the walk—that's a strong culture.

After five years at Vanguard, I was semi-retired. I left the firm and thought about what I could do next. I wasn't swimming in money, but I was comfortable. I lived in a little one-bedroom apartment in a building I owned, while renting out the other units. I attribute this time in my life to Robert Kiyosaki's board game, Cashflow. The goal of that game was to get out of the rat race. I decided to play that game in real life, and it took me about three years to get out of the rat race. My expenses that were not covered by passive income were about $400 a month, all in. I figured out that I could work 10 hours a week at Starbucks and get health insurance, if I really wanted to, in order to cover those expenses. Obviously, I was in my early 20s, not thinking about how I would pay for a family.

I still love Vanguard as a company, but I wasn't inspired there. When I looked at my boss's boss's boss, I knew that was not who I wanted to be in 30 years. A lot of people in the company were inspired by cutting costs and being the lowest cost provider. I realized that I wanted to do something different. I wanted to innovate and do something to help people from what I had to offer, even though I didn't yet know what that was. I decided that if I want to get from point A to point B, and I find myself getting too comfortable on a path that is not going to take me to point B, that's when I intuitively stop. I could see my future, and it wasn't what I wanted. I was too comfortable.

Everyone thought I was crazy, and would tell me that you can't have a mid-life crisis in your 20s! But I wanted to do something big. I wanted to affect more people. I've seen people get caught in certain patterns or wavelengths while 10 or 20 years pass. Whatever they thought they wanted to do, they no longer have time for. They get stuck in the normal pattern of life and they no longer have a choice.

This period when I was searching for something bigger became an exercise of my faith. I spent a lot of time in prayer. I took a trip to Israel. I thought long and hard about what was next in my life. Sure, if I had accepted the life I had at Vanguard, it wouldn't be a bad life. I have many friends who still work there and live happy lives. And many are more well off financially than me. But I also realized at the time when I was contemplating my future, that my version of happiness was different from that of my friends at Vanguard.

One afternoon, I found myself at the gym with a bunch of 60- and 70-year-old retired guys. They asked me, "What do you do, Adam?" I told them I was semi-retired, and they responded, "What do you mean? You can't just stop in your 20s. You have to do more with your life. You can't just sit around with us smoking cigars. We're three times your age. Get a job. Do something." I went home feeling a little guilty, so I put in one application to Charles Schwab. I thought it was a great company, because whenever I lost business at Vanguard, it was always to Schwab. Since both are really great companies, I would check out the competition.

The interview was great, but I wasn't completely sold. On my drive home, the manager called and offered me the job, which is not something that company normally does. Between the guys at the gym, and now this, I knew God was guiding me. I had to take the job. Since I already had my Series 6 and 63 licenses, this job would be a way to get my Series 7, and also propel me forward in the financial industry.

I started in the call center in Phoenix, and worked on various teams, from the active trader team to the overnight desk. A series of promotions within the company led me to California, where I worked in the branch network. This move turned out to be a great experience. One major thing Schwab taught me about was innovation.

At the end of my time working there, I began to see I could be a financial advisor for the next 30 years and retire, except under the Schwab model, I wouldn't have any equity. I won't own anything. Again, I knew I wasn't headed to the right point B I had envisioned.

I ruined everything I had going for me within Schwab to start from scratch. Again. I left Schwab to start my own company, Century City Wealth Management. And at the same time, I started another company, called Mr. Century City, which was a way for me to publish my first book. It also was how I got started in the media business.

I self-published my first book, which I have left on Amazon to prove that anyone can publish a book. At that time, I was still a financial advisor and I thought I'd use the book as a calling card. I handed it out and it did get me business, because people knew my story. However, it also intrigued my colleagues and they began asking me to help them write a book. When the third successful business owner in six months asked me to help him write a book, I had to say, "Okay, God, I got it. I'll figure out this book thing. Thank you." I had to figure out a business I knew nothing about, but it turned out I had a knack for it.

From that point, my media business started to grow rapidly. I realized I couldn't do both my wealth management business and the media business. That's when I chose to close Century City Wealth Management, in order to pursue full time what is now the media company we call Mission Matters. I am who I am today, not because I had a master plan. I never had a master plan. Most of my story is about me saying yes to opportunities that showed up, which is why I call myself the accidental entrepreneur.

Chapter Two

The Serial Entrepreneur

– Elliot Kallen

"It doesn't matter how many times you have failed. You only have to be right once."

~Mark Cuban

A serial entrepreneur is someone who likes to start something. They like to build businesses. They get excited about growth and building momentum. They want to create their own company. And they're not satisfied with just one. They want to build a second and a third. They are also visionaries and risk-takers, with a capacity for discipline thrown in the mix. I definitely resemble this description. We could debate whether these characteristics are inborn or forged by life experiences. Most likely, it's a bit of both.

Both of my parents strongly influenced my life in different ways. My mother was an Auschwitz survivor. Being the child of an Auschwitz survivor automatically bestows upon you massive amounts of guilt. She was an old-fashioned European mom. She grew up in Vienna, Austria, where mothers raised kids and dads made money. She was the driver of education in our family, always pushing us to do better. If I got 95-percent on a test, she would ask me if anybody got 100-percent. I hear her words in my head all the time, which I think is a good sign as an entrepreneur. If something didn't work yesterday, I know I can do better today. Due to my upbringing, I feel that's why entrepreneurs don't really fail—they just learn lessons, then do better.

When I was a kid, my mother was a big fan of the Kennedy family. Today, she would be called a moderate, but back then, she was called a liberal. What she admired about old Joe Kennedy was that he read the newspaper to his kids at night, and then they discussed politics. When I was in the seventh grade, she would buy Newsweek or Time, and my brother and I would have to read an article, and then debate it. Of course, the topics of the 1970s included women's rights, abortion and the Vietnam War. My brother took one side, and I took the other. My mother was the moderator, and my dad was the judge. The debate could never be personal, and the following night we had to switch sides. I've argued abortion on both sides probably 50 times. My mom wanted her two boys to be international attorneys.

While at school, we would learn French and German. We studied law, ethics, credibility and critical thinking. My Mother really pushed critical thinking. She wanted us to be capable of talking about subjects objectively and passionately, but not emotionally. My mother hated mass thinking, which is very understandable after her experience during World War II.

In college, I didn't hear my mother's voice at all. My mom was sick, and my dad was dying. I was an immature young man focused more on making money instead of trying to improve myself. I saw two roads I could take in college. One would be to get a master's degree in something I really liked, which was economics. Then, there was the road that would lead to an instant job and instant money, which was accounting. I didn't really like accounting, but I had a vision of getting my CPA, then becoming the CFO of a company. And eventually I would become the president of IT&T, a huge company right there in New Jersey.

When I shared this with my dad, he said, "You don't have the personality to be an accountant. If you like economics, study that. But you're a businessman." I've always had a big, outgoing and friendly personality. And I'm very non-judgmental. It doesn't matter to me what you do, where you went to school or where your family line is from. You are my friend. Come here, and let me give you a hug. Let's talk. To this day, I have that personality. Dad saw it. I didn't. And because of that, I didn't listen to him.

Entrepreneurs sometimes make quick decisions for the wrong reasons. They make them, because they are quick. And that is exactly what I did. I made a very quick, major decision for the wrong reason. That became one of those life lessons about why entrepreneurs fail. Entrepreneurship practically requires an ability to make quick decisions. Unfortunately, many of those decisions are not necessarily the right decisions.

As soon as I graduated and started working as an accountant, I thought, uh oh, this is a bad idea. I don't like this at all. I'm not a sit down at a desk kind of guy. I'm a get up and talk guy. I remember that I had a summer job, where I was graded on keystrokes. I got a 25-cent raise, because I did 10,000 keystrokes per minute. I did not like that. There was no intellect involved, just rote numbers. When you get hired as an auditor, you become a bean counter. "You say you have 52 widgets and the sheet says you have 51. Where's the other one?" That's so not me.

I talked to my dad about it, and he said, "Quit. I know a really good business you can get into. I'll help you. I know a little bit about the ink and solvent business. Let's work together." We took over a basically defunct company and decided to turn it around. Unfortunately, after two heart attacks, my dad became incapacitated 90 days into this venture, so I was on my own.

Inks and solvents were interesting, but when I looked at the business, I realized that all the products were being used in warehouses and factories. They were not being used in offices at all. Since it was a blue-collar field, I asked myself what else these people needed. Since I was out there talking to people, trying to build up the business, I discovered what they needed was tape, boxes and custom packaging. That's when I realized we could add more products. I converted the company into an industrial packaging and shipping supply company. Then I began to realize that we had reps working for us. I thought, why do I have these reps? I can bring in employees and they will be 100-percent dedicated to me.

Over the next five years, we became a 35-person company with over $5 million in sales. We grew tenfold in five years. I was very good at managing sales, but unfortunately, I didn't have the wherewithal to manage cash flow. That was a huge lesson for me as a business owner starting out. Accounting is just adding numbers. Cash flow, growth projections and banking—that's CFO level stuff. I didn't yet understand any of that. I thought having a 20-percent or 25-percent net profit, you put all that back into the business. However, running a small business, you've got payables, receivables, payroll, inventory—and everybody else gets paid before you get paid. When the economic slowdown of 1987 hit, my receivables went from 40-days to 90-days. But I still had to pay for my inventory, and we hit a major cash flow wall. Here I was in my mid-20s, owing half a million dollars, plus the mortgage on my house.

Uncontrolled growth is a problem for a lot of small business owners. Many wonder, if I'm growing at such a fast rate, why don't I have more money? I'm making all this money. Where is it? Well, it's going into growth. It's going into salaries. You hire people every day and some of them don't work out. That's dead money. You increase inventory and some of it gets sold, but some of it just sits there while your payables keep coming in. Payables, overhead and insurance costs are all going up by the minute. Did you project out properly for all of that? You have to figure out exactly what you need to run your business.

It's important to understand, if you are just starting out in business, to sit down with someone who knows what you're doing, and put some cash-flow projections together, according to what you may need, based on different situations. A good business accountant will be able to help you out with that.

Meanwhile, as a small business owner who was in a financial crisis, I realized that my wife and I needed a solution to our problem.

Nowadays, we have venture capitalists. But in the old days, the New York Times had a section called "Venture Needed." You put an ad in the paper, and people called you from all over the world saying, "I've got capital, tell me about your business." If they wanted to invest, they may say, "I'll take 49-percent of your company, here's a million dollars." Those were the kinds of offers I was getting. But the feeling I had was that they didn't want the 49-percent, they instead wanted me to default, so I could give them this profitable entity and they could run it.

My wife and I were really torn at the time. We didn't know what to do, and our stress levels were through the roof. One day, we went to a New York Jets game and literally sat in the stands arguing about it all afternoon. We realized at the end of the day, we missed the entire game, and that it was time to exit the company.

Due to the debt, the company didn't have enough value to sell outright, so I sold the assets to my sales manager, who wanted to buy the company. He could pay me over a certain time period, so I restructured the debt and used the cash flow to pay it off over time.

It took a few months to wind it down, close the building, clean it up and leave it in good shape. Then I started looking for positions. In those days, you looked for jobs in the newspaper. I went to interviews for about five months, and I could never figure out why I couldn't get hired. I came close several times, only to be rejected in the end. It was extremely frustrating.

There are outplacement firms that test executives for skills, and I thought that would work for an entrepreneur like me, as well. I went to one in Philadelphia, where I met a guy with a PhD, who was the head of the community college there. After a series of tests, he told me the reason I wasn't getting hired was because I was a threat to people, and that I should go back into business for myself. He said, "You need to figure out what business you want to get into. And don't think about a business for the next 30 years. Think about a business for the next five years." That was good advice. I needed to figure out how to make an above average living, or even a good living, then figure out if that was short-term or long-term.

The overall take away from my assessment was that there's a part of my personality that is not just an entrepreneur. I'm a serial entrepreneur. I like starting and building, which is what he saw in me. I could easily start, build and sell, then go start another business. There's nothing wrong with that. They just don't teach you that in college. If I was in college, they would call that person a failure. Today, we call them a serial entrepreneur. Elon Musk started and grew PayPal, and when he was done with that, he bought and grew Tesla. He's a serial entrepreneur. If you said you were going to do that in college, they would tell you that's a recipe for failure.

After learning this about myself, my next step was to start a commercial environmental supply business selling air and water remediation products. We sold products that took particles out of air, and out of commercial and residential water. I remember when Love Canal, a neighborhood in Niagara Falls, N.Y., became the site of an enormous environmental disaster in the 1970s. Decades of toxic chemical dumping had to be cleaned up over the course of more than 20 years by a government superfund operation. There was a lot of superfund money, and cleaning up the environment was a hot topic at the time. It was an opportunity I wanted to work on. I started that company, and soon had about 100 reps around the country, marketing our products.

By 1992, almost all of the superfund money was gone, and the topic was no longer on people's minds. I then started looking around for something else I could do. I love dealing with business owners. They are the people I've dealt with my whole life, and the people I'm most comfortable with. I'm not really a kitchen table kind of guy. I didn't want to sell cemetery plots or life insurance. I asked myself what business owners needed. I thought they could use some help with investments and financial planning. Maybe commercial insurance. Capital. Maybe I could develop some type of venture capital help. Who could I do that with, and who can train me on that? I secured myself interviews with companies like Lincoln Financial, Merrill Lynch, EF Hutton and Shearson Lehman, all on the East Coast. They wanted me to be a telemarketer for the first couple of years, while I built my book of business. But that's not me.

Meanwhile, my wife, who grew up in California, got pregnant. After several miscarriages, she used to say to me, "If I ever get pregnant past the third month, can we move to California?" On the way home from the doctor's office, after she passed the third month with twins, she reminded me of my promise. We moved to Northern California, across the bay from San Francisco. Shortly before moving, my wife handed me a San Francisco Chronicle with a noticeable ad for Lincoln Financial, which I was already familiar with from New Jersey.

Lincoln was one of those firms with an interesting process and mediocre management. But I called them up and the recruiter was also from New York, so we hit it off really well. By luck, our new house was just a few miles from their office. They kept me in the interview for eight hours, where we worked out a deal. They had me start with the idea of eventually building their business division. Since Lincoln didn't have one, that's what I did.

In 1999, I decided to part ways with Lincoln, but it was very amicable. Many of the people who continue to work there are still my friends today. I started my own firm after leaving the company, and I've been providing financial services to business owners ever since.

Those were the early days of my serial entrepreneurship. I didn't start out knowing that's who I would become. I had to figure it out along the way. I got a lucky break when I found the guy who proved to me beyond a shadow of a doubt that entrepreneurship was for me. I followed the breadcrumbs that life dropped onto my path, but I also took the initiative to forge ahead, full force, once I coalesced my vision for controlling my own destiny.

Chapter Three

Meeting in the Metaverse

– Adam Torres

"Life is beautiful, not because of the things we see or do. Life is beautiful, because of the people we meet."

~Simon Sinek

One of my mentors told me that when you're really focused on what you're doing professionally, you tend to only associate with people you are working with, either clients or employees. You don't usually have much time for anything else. Throughout my various careers, I've found that to be true. Whenever I was trying to build something big, my identity became attached to whatever I was building, and my social life circled around the work I was doing.

The first time I talk to most people is when they appear on my show. It's a pretty cool way to connect with people, because I get to really understand them and make that connection while interviewing them. I also have a record of most of the people I talk to, because I have the interview. What started as a joke within our company, has become a reality—my contact list is our website. If I want to find a person or company, I go to MissionMatters.com and type in what I'm looking for in the search box. More than 5,000 interviews later, there aren't too many industries we haven't covered.

I began meeting people and building relationships online back when I was in college, which was when Facebook just came out. Back then, to be on Facebook, you had to be in college and have a legitimate college email address. I remember meeting students around the country, who were also in my fraternity. When we went on road trips to different college campuses, I got to know some of the people I met online, in person. I have even built lifelong relationships with some of them and I still know them today.

For my generation, many people have been able to forge meaningful relationships online, most of which become personal. However, that wasn't possible for previous generations. My generation was able to witness the transition of possibility in the world and it has been remarkable. It has shown just how remarkable it is when thinking about the world during and post COVID-19 pandemicPeople have become more willing to do business and build relationships entirely online with people they may never meet in person.

At Mission Matters, I have employees and contractors who live all over the world, from the Philippines to Argentina, from London to New York and from Texas to Florida. I have been working with many of them for years, though we have never met in person. Mission Matters has always been a virtual online business. In fact, I have probably spent more hours with these people than my own family, because we spend so much time working, as many small businesses tend to do.

There was a time when people assumed the best person for a job was the person right in front of them. But today, the best software engineer to help you launch your product or app might not be the person in your hometown. It could be someone in Eastern Europe, or someone across the world, who is better and more adept at doing your project and offering the best price point. This accessibility of talent should speed up the pace of innovation, remove old biases and do a lot for diversity, equity and inclusion.

One of the perks to working long distance or over a platform like Zoom, is that you don't get the same feelings about people as when they are right in front of you. You may evaluate people much more on their work, which you review in advance of a meeting, versus relying on a first impression when someone walks into a room. The ability to develop and grow professional relationships online is important, which is exactly what I have done with my co-author, Elliot Kallen.

I believe the ability to develop and grow great professional relationships online is important for humanity and innovation. There are people around the world who are working on some of the same problems as you or I have in our companies. While y might be ahead, they might have the missing piece, or vice versa. The ability of two people to find each other and to connect has significant opportunities, and when you think about the limitless possibilities of a global company concept that creates so many more chances to change the world through business. And when you meet the right global people who give you a push in the right direction, there's no limit to what you can create.

I never really had any inclination to write about the Mission Matters story and what we are doing, until Elliot suggested it. I met Elliot the way I meet most people ... he was a guest on my show. He was a really fun guest and we hit it off immediately. Soon after, he had me as a guest on his show: *Meet the Expert with Elliot Kallen*, which is available on all the big platforms, including Apple, Amazon, Google and iHeart.

After I was on his show, our mutually important friendship grew even more. That led us to doing a book together, called *Mission Matters Business Leaders Edition, Volume 5, by Adam Torres and Elliot Kallen*. Elliot and I worked together to assemble a collection of authors from the business community for a co-authored book, where participants shared their stories of triumph and sometimes defeat. It was a tour de force of entrepreneurs using their resources and ingenuity to not only maintain cash flow during the pandemic, but also provide much needed services to save their businesses and save lives.

Elliot's own chapter in the book, *The REAL Secret to Success: Leading with Humanity*, demonstrates his character and values, which make him great to work with, and it shows that he truly cares about the people he works with daily. He models humility in everything he does. He leads with good humor as well. Giving back to the communities he cares about is central to his company's culture, as well as his personal life.

We enjoyed the process of working together so much, we decided to write a full book together, the one you're currently holding in your hands. That was a big step, because writing a full book together is a huge commitment. It requires a lot of time working together, just to get it done. Then, you have to work together to promote it. What it comes down to is that you have to really like each other, which I hope permeates throughout this book.

There has to be a certain chemistry and a rhythm to the way you work, which allows you to stick with someone long enough to achieve that goal. It's one thing to work with someone on an interview, or a chapter or a smaller project. But for a large book project, you really have to like the person.

For over a year and a half of working together, Elliot and I had never met in person, only online. Elliot lives in Northern California, and I live in Southern California. However, recently he was vacationing in Santa Barbara, so we split the difference and met in Malibu, at the beautiful Sunset Restaurant. Elliot brought his lovely wife, Tammy, and I brought our Director of Marketing, Jennifer Chen. We had a fun lunch together and it was great to meet in person, after doing so much work together virtually during the pandemic.

COVID-19 was an interesting time for everyone, but especially for businesses. Some businesses grew quickly, while others struggled or went out of business. As a media person, I had a unique vantage point during that time. While everything shut down, including the sporting events, teams, restaurants and cinemas, we were busier than ever. The demand for our content skyrocketed, and for quite a while, we were the only producer in town for our type of content.

When the pandemic began, I had some friends who were living abroad, who let me know what was going on in China long before the shutdown happened here. I decided to quarantine myself about a month before anyone knew what was happening in the United States. Since I interview people all day, I couldn't risk getting sick and not being able to do that. It would have been a risk to the company, because if I was not able to work, it would have halted a large part of our content production.

During the two years of the pandemic, I probably did a thousand interviews. We did not stop. We just kept going. The calls and leads continued to roll in and we kept producing content.

The people I interviewed fell into a few categories. One was the entrepreneur, who found ways to use their current resources to reposition their company in the marketplace, in order to meet the demands needed at that time. For example, there was a graphic design shop that normally did signs and displays. However, when everything closed, those types of orders stopped. The company pivoted during the pandemic and started making Plexiglas dividers for places like grocery stores and hospitals. Based on that need, the company ended up growing significantly.

There were also a lot of savvy entrepreneurs, who were trying to help others. They weren't doing it from an opportunistic standpoint. They were only looking around for work, so they could keep their people employed. They figured out a product they could make, using their current resources that were in demand. They were able to help others and they were rewarded. Quite a few people I interviewed were in that category. One of the reasons they wanted to come on the show was to share how they pivoted and what they had been doing to help others during the pandemic.

Some entrepreneurs, especially people in the event business, were not able to figure out how to pivot and change their business strategies before their cash flow and reserves ran out. Unfortunately, they went out of business.

Yet another segment of entrepreneurs I interviewed already had been quite successful and they were trying to hang onto what they had created. They were in industries that were not conducive to a pivot, such as financial advisors. It's hard to sell that kind of a service when people are paralyzed and don't want to make major personal and financial decisions, because they don't know what's going to happen in the world. While financial advisors can find different ways to serve their clients, it doesn't mean they're going to grow.

That said, some financial advisors were able to pivot to online services, and some grew tremendously. Elliot kept his offices open, because the State of California deemed them essential services. Not everyone wanted to come in, but those who did had that option, and that made Elliot's business resourceful and a pivotal presence during the pandemic.

I'm always amazed by the ingenuity and resourcefulness of entrepreneurs, especially ones like Elliot Kallen. He has a lot of wisdom to share, and he does it with humility and a great sense of humor.

PART TWO

MISSION-BASED ENTREPRENEURSHIP

MR. CENTURY CITY, LLC

CHAPTER FOUR

WITHOUT VISION, NOTHING HAPPENS

– ELLIOT KALLEN

"A vision is not just a picture of what could be; it is an appeal to our better selves, a call to become something more."

~Rosabeth Moss Kanter

L ife can sometimes resemble a carnival fun house of disorienting mirrors. It's easy to get lost temporarily. Having a vision for your future, provides a steadying North Star to help keep you on track, when the clowns in your life try to obfuscate reality.

I believe every great idea begins with a vision, and business is no different. Without a vision, we can get stuck focusing on today and not giving enough thought about tomorrow. Great entrepreneurs have dreams about their vision, and they know in their hearts they are going in the right direction.

When I was in college, I had various jobs every weekend. I managed a parking lot, worked for a caterer as well as a laborer in construction. I was one of the few college kids who had money in the bank. But the sacrifices were all those weekend parties my friends were going to, because I wasn't going with them. And those sacrifices affected my whole attitude toward Rutgers University for years.

My brother and sister lived in dorms, but I lived off campus so I could work. It was a very disparate experience. Sometimes, money motivation is a temporary motivation with no long-term vision associated with it. I've heard about people selling their Super Bowl rings, because they needed to pay for something right at that moment, which is really bad. They've gotten themselves into a position where they can't eat or pay rent. That's when "the right now" can be your enemy, because "the right now" always lacks vision.

It's also true that if you're not living in "the right now," you're living in dreamland. But if you're only living in "the right now," then tomorrow will be the same thing as today. For you to get better and move to a different circumstance in your life, you need to have a vision. You have to be going somewhere. If not, you're only living for "the right now." Every day, you can go to work and make $23 an hour. Tomorrow you can do the same thing. Next Thursday, same thing. In five years, guess what you can still do?

People with vision step back, and say, "One day, I'm going to own that company. How do I do that?" They create a vision. They start working on that vision more and more. Your vision gets you out of "the right now." However, if your vision lacks grounding, it might put you in fantasyland, which may or may not be a good thing. It's interesting to note, some of the biggest companies in the world were joke visions from someone's college days.

The foremost vision I've had was when I came to California and began working in the financial services business. I immediately had a vision of owning my own company and building it from the ground up. I wanted to figure out how to make it a national company one day. Every day, when I came to work, my head was in my vision. The first assistant I hired at Lincoln, Yvette, is still with me 30 years later,and she tells everyone the story about her interview with me. She remembers me telling her, "Listen, I just want you to know, I work for Lincoln. But in just a few years, we're going to be starting our own company, and we're going to develop into a national company." I don't remember saying it, but she remembers it like it was yesterday.

My ex-wife and my family used to tell me that they all know I'm working with Lincoln and have a dream to own my own firm someday, but they would also tell me that I need to get a job somewhere, because I have two little kids at home. At that time, I had newborn twins, so I went on several job interviews while I was at Lincoln. Every interview would convince me to stay focused on what I was doing and not lose my vision. I arduously stayed where I was, and it paid off.

Those were my painful and lean years. When you start from scratch in the financial industry, it's a really hard way to make a living. I don't wish it on anyone. To make $40,000 a year, you have to sell a million dollars' worth of products. That's a big number when you don't know anybody and you're starting from scratch. Most of my initial clients were giving me $2,000, $5,000 or $10,000. At that time, $50,000 was a huge amount of money. Today, $50,000 is below my minimum. There are people who have been doing this for 15 or 20 years and they manage $20 million dollars. If you make 1-percent, that's $200,000 a year before you pay your overhead and staff. Maybe you walk away with $100,000. Where are you going to live in California on $100,000 a year?

Another aspect of working for someone else meant that I didn't get to decide what I sold. When I started out at Lincoln, I was doing money management, selling life and medical insurance products, as well as 401k plans. Lincoln management came to me one day and said they needed me to stop selling medical plans and 401ks, and instead focus on insurance. When I asked why, they told me that's where the money is made.

I was building a business around business owners who needed medical and 401ks, but Lincoln wasn't interested in that. My group within Lincoln built a small division that eventually became Prosperity Financial Group. We walked away with the whole thing, because Lincoln management didn't want it. They didn't understand it. Their market was not the business owner. Their market was selling life insurance. They understood selling a $5 million dollar insurance policy to take care of your taxes and protect your family when you died. They lacked vision. Like so many companies out there, they have been around long enough to have the momentum to get the same business, over and over.

The vision I created for my financial services business had three arms, all of which dealt with business owners. There was personal investing, employee benefits and insurance products. I stayed very focused on that. I originally wanted to bring in a partner for each one of those areas, but it didn't work out that way, because partners have different ideas.

Having a vision is not a guarantee that things will work out for you. When you have a vision, that vision will be tested. You can begin to lose your vision when you're being tested, because there are a multitude of distractions. For me, the number one distraction was my divorce. Because I am so family centric, the thought of losing my family was devastating. Unfortunately, when people go through divorces, they tend to bleed on everyone around them. It was not pretty. I didn't realize I had been allowing my personal problem to affect my work, until my business partner communicated it to me.

When my marriage started to spiral downward, due to my wife's depression, I started to lose my vision of where we were going. I became too negative. Every day was negative. I didn't want to take it out on my kids. I also didn't want to take it out on my soon to be ex-wife, because that is really unhealthy and stupid things happen when you do that. So, I discharged that negativity playing hockey.

Every free moment I had, I played ice hockey as a goalie. I banged on my steering wheel all the way there, and all the way home, so I could leave my negativity behind me. It was a great release, but when I came to work, I still couldn't get my mind to focus. It seems like whenever you have something medical or emotional, like a divorce or a parent dying, it can throw you totally out of whack and make you lose your focus. That's why having a strong vision of your career path is so important, because it is something to hold onto when your world gets rocked.

Creating a vision is something I would recommend for every entrepreneur. The trick is to protect your vision from life's distractions. Write it down and stick it in front of you, so you can see it all the time. Put it on your computer. I actually have a goal sheet that I laminated and put in the shower. It has personal, business, family, kids' and spousal visions. My wife laughs at me, because the first vision she wanted me to commit to was making sure I always maintain great communication with her. That and taking us on a great vacation every year.

My business visions include how many new clients I want each month. When I look at my vision sheet, I'm thinking that I want to make sure this happens. I want to make sure this turns into revenue. I look at the numbers, because what I do about them is the one thing I have control over. I'm not in control of a recession or a 30-percent drop in the equity markets, but I am in control of what I do.

There's a famous prayer, asking God for the serenity to accept what I cannot change, the courage to change what I can and the wisdom to know the difference. I think part of being an entrepreneur is understanding what you have the power to change, and what you don't have the power to change. During my divorce, it was my attitude, which was in question. I was very aware of my actions, not hers, while going through the divorce. Mine, I could control. Hers, I just had to deal with, which is easier said than done.

Whether you're getting a divorce, fighting cancer or heart disease, or losing a parent, each one of those life changes are hard. When you are stuck in a negative emotion, it is important to have your visions and aspirations written down and in front of you—in your car, in the shower, above your toilet or on your nightstand. These visual reminders can really help you keep your focus. It also helps to hire a consultant or counselor. If you have someone to share your vision with, who can also help keep you on track, that's great, too. It makes you responsible to someone else, during times when you won't be responsible to yourself. When you have accountability to another person, you act differently.

Something that really brought me through my divorce and the recession was talking through my problems, and realizing that if I didn't change the way I was reacting, then I was not going to be a great dad, which was always my number one vision. My number one vision has never been money. It has always been family first. Make sure to understand your visions and keep them in focus.

When you have visions, you can begin to work backwards and figure out how to bring them to fruition. Have a business vision. It may not be completely in focus at first, but as you keep focusing, it will become clearer. It will also evolve. When I started Prosperity Financial Group, in 1993, my vision was not what I have today. My business is now bigger and more profitable. I can now afford to turn away business that is outside what I specialize in. When I started, if someone had $2,000 and could fog a mirror, they could be my client.

One of the things that helped me in my earlier years in business was attending various seminars. I remember Stephen Covey saying, "Begin with the end in mind." Most people get stuck in the middle, or they have no vision at all. My kids once said to me, "The secret to being a successful entrepreneur is hard work." I explained to them that those guys who pick up our garbage work really hard. The janitor at the high school busts his chops to keep that school clean. Security guards work hard, but they're in a dead-end world.

Maybe that's enough for them, but if you want to be an entrepreneur, you can't sit in the middle of a dead-end opportunity. You have to think about where you're going. What's your vision? It doesn't have to be set in stone. Lots of people have failed on the way to success. Former presidents have had failures and even bankruptcies. However, they stayed true to their vision and kept working. They didn't give up.

When I think back to my packaging business, a part of me feels like it failed. But as an entrepreneur, I choose to look at it as a learning experience. It was one bloody nose on my road to success.

There's a difference between the battle and the war. In this world, we have battles every day. Some in health, some in marriage or some in work. But the war is a whole different conversation. You may lose a battle, but the war isn't lost until you give up. You can regroup and get your troops back together, but don't lose your vision.

Your vision may change. What I did in the 1980s, and what I do in the 2020s are very different. As we evolve our vision, we have to evolve as leaders, as well.

If you want to be a really good entrepreneur, write all of your visions down and put them somewhere you will see them every day. Now, mine starts with a spousal vision. I also have a family vision, a business vision, an ethics vision, and a character vision. Five visions on one page.

My business vision declares how much money I will make and how many new clients I will bring in. I divided those numbers for the year into monthly numbers. I regularly ask myself, am I meeting those numbers?

When thinking about how my vision affects my business, it is important for me to enlist my coworkers. So, I gave my marketing director a copy of that breakdown. He now walks into my office and asks me if I'm making my phone calls so we can hit our vision. Everybody is on track and asking if we are all doing what we need to do to support each other in what we need to do.

It wasn't always like this. I just have people who get it now.

CHAPTER FIVE

JUST GET STARTED

– ADAM TORRES

"The way to get started is to quit talking and begin doing."

~Walt Disney

When my co-founder, Chirag Sagar, and I started our company, it was called Money Matters Top Tips. That was our brand and we were dedicated solely to book publishing. I was still a financial advisor and trying to wear two hats, one as a financial advisor and the other as a book publisher.

Money Matters Top Tips morphed and developed into Mission Matters, which is now a multifaceted media company with a podcasting, publishing, marketing and advertising division. Think of it like a Forbes, but our whole concept is around being a mission-based media outlet. We showcase and amplify business owners, leaders, entrepreneurs and executives. Our goal is to tell the stories that need to be told, but are not being prioritized by mainstream media.

There are many interesting people who are accomplished individuals, and who don't have time to sit down and write a book. We feel strongly that their valuable knowledge gets lost, which is why we publish and promote the best of the best in each of their varied fields. That's one division of the company.

Another division of the company is our Mission Matters Podcast Network where we recruit, train, develop and distribute podcast shows for clients. Think of it like a record label. A record label signs an artist. They do all the work on the backend and it's the artist's job to record the music. We do the exact same thing with podcast shows. We do all the distribution like any other traditional media company.

Podcasting is our thing, and something I spend a lot of my time invested in and working on. We have launched more than 150 different shows so far, we have produced more than 6,000 episodes and at least 75,000 pieces of content. On the book publishing side of the business, we have published at least 300 authors now. The main idea is to amplify stories. That's our tagline and that's what we do.

What I have found in this journey of helping other people to tell their story is that without us, many people would never share their knowledge and backgrounds or even feel like their message needed to be heard. That is direct feedback from some of our podcast hosts. They say, "If it wasn't for the Podcast Network, I would never host a podcast." Some of that is because we handle the technical aspects for people who don't want to learn how to edit or manage distribution. But another side of that is having the encouragement of a community, where everyone is rooting for each other and helping get their content out there. That's a big piece of what we are doing right now. As we have gotten bigger and helped more people expand their reach with the content we manage and create, I don't even think I understand the magnitude of what we are building, in terms of the amount of content and stories we are producing every day. I believe what we are doing now will affect generations to come.

Everything we do is directed toward expanding the reach of high-caliber clients, so they can share their knowledge with not only the next generation of business leaders, but also with current business leaders. Creating that brain trust of knowledge is the real goal that goes well beyond my lifetime. Our passion for the work we do is rooted in who we are at Mission Matters.

We are not an influencer brand. We could easily invest marketing dollars into making my name bigger or making Adam the face of the company. However, that's not our goal and it's not our ethics. Even my interview style is to intentionally take a back seat in the interview. I make sure to ask a lot of questions, and try not to talk more than 20-percent of the interview. I make sure our guest is doing the talking. It's a different interviewing style from a lot of the current popularized media, which is how I want it to be, so the focus is always on the person being interviewed.

For the compilation books that we publish, there's a reason I only write the introduction. The books aren't for me to position myself as an influencer, or even as a business leader or thought leader. We focus on getting our authors' names out there, not mine.

I remember before we started the Mission Matters book series, the very first book I wrote was all me. I could have continued down that path and written more books, building myself as a brand and a speaker. Instead, Chirag and I thought about how to tell the stories of others. How do we amplify their mission and their brand? That's when we came up with the co-author model, bringing together a group of talented leaders and authors, who wouldn't otherwise have the expertise to write and market a book.

When I wrote my first book, I didn't even know what a copyeditor was. I didn't know how graphic designers worked. I didn't realize you had to get the interior of the book designed as well as the cover. I had no idea how the entire process came together to create a book. My production copy of my first book was beginner level, at best. But I leave it out there intentionally, not because we can't republish it. We're a professional publishing company now and could easily rebrand it and upgrade it to fit our quality of content. The reason I leave it out there is because I want people to know that anyone can publish a book—and you should.

I believe everyone has a story inside them that is worth telling. Whenever anyone tells me that they don't know if they have a story in them, and they don't know if they can publish a book, I show them my first one. It's my ugly duckling. I tell them I wrote it by talking into a phone on a train while I was traveling. I told some stories from my experiences and sent them to an editor. They put it together and like magic, a book came out. You can still find it on Amazon under the title: ***Money Matters: 21 Practical Lessons for Everyday Success, by Adam Torres***.

Even though it was an ugly duckling, the content was good, because it's my story. And our entire company has since grown out of that first book. I truly believe that whoever was meant to hear that story will gravitate to it. And if they were not meant to read it, they are just not our readers. Without that first book, our company would not exist. Those 300 authors wouldn't have been published. And we wouldn't have produced more than 40,000 pieces of content.

My ugly duckling is what attracted people to the idea of writing a book of their own. People started to approach me and ask me to help them publish a book, which was amazing. I said yes to them, and figured out how to help them as I went.

The reason we started the podcast was to sell more books. I didn't even want to do a podcast. My co-founder Chirag, said, "Adam, you have to do a podcast." We needed to sell books and we needed to figure out how to create other content. I was concerned about starting another business, because we didn't know how to do it, but we figured it out, and before we knew it, I had hundreds of episodes recorded. And of course, as I interviewed people, they naturally asked, "How can I start a podcast?"

Speaking of ugly ducklings, my first show was beginner level as well. Even before the podcast, I had a show called The Gratitude Show. I was so scared to be in front of a camera that I only asked one question. I would live-stream on Periscope, and as people tuned in, I'd ask them, "What are you grateful for?" It wasn't even a two-way conversation. I was just reading the chat. I did 300 episodes asking people, "What are you grateful for today? Being grateful is important. I want to hear what you're grateful for." And some random listener would write, "I'm grateful for my family." So I would respond, "Awesome, John. Why are you grateful for your family?"

I soon had thousands of people watching that show from around the world, as far away as Saudi Arabia. I remember one particular story, where a woman was telling me she was a computer software engineer and programmer. She was the first woman in Saudi Arabia to ever earn that certification. They had just opened that program up to women. I really cheered her on.

Years later, people would find me on Twitter and other platforms who remembered that original show. I'd get invites all around the world, just from doing that little Gratitude Show. I was so scared to do it, because there was no production to it. I just went live and said, "Gratitude Show, Episode One. What are you grateful for?" Then, Episode Two. And eventually, "Hey, if this is your first time here, I just ask people what are you grateful for." I was surprised by the responses and engagement. If people weren't engaging, I'd say, "What? You're not going to participate? Come on! You've got to tell us what you're grateful for, otherwise everybody's just going to sit here, watching me do nothing the whole show." I did that for a half hour and people would listen.

My mission at that time was to spread positivity. Eventually, people wanted to see the show on YouTube, because Periscope wasn't really a mainstream platform. The transition to that platform was difficult. I probably had one of the rockiest starts on YouTube ever. If I thought Periscope was difficult, YouTube was like getting a PhD in content creation. I recorded 10 to 15 five-minute episodes a weekend, then I would schedule them out for the whole month. We released an episode a day for almost a year.

The cool part of the YouTube show was that I would give people missions. I might say, "Today's mission is … I want everyone to text someone you love and tell them you're grateful for them. And leave in the comment section what happened." I got amazing comments and even text messages from people I knew personally. One guy said, "My wife was crying. She said she hasn't heard me say something like that to her in years."

When I started my podcast, I used regular headphones and my iPhone 6 for my first almost 1,000 episodes. I talked to people for 10 or 15 minutes and posted it. I didn't know what I was doing. They were regular conversations, but people really liked them.

That's when we started to get overwhelmed, to the point where I didn't think I could be a financial advisor anymore. I was spending so much time with my podcast and engaging with the listeners that juggling the show and my financial advisor obligations became difficult. There was so much demand to be on the show that we started to get backed up. We had more than 50 episodes that hadn't been released. Even if we put out one per day, it would take months to get them all out. We made a huge decision and we released them all at once. Surprisingly, our per-episode downloads went up, not down. You would think there would be fewer listens, because we released so much content. But the opposite was true for us. Chirag and I were shocked at the outcome, but grateful for the support.

At one point, it became ridiculous. We were releasing 80 episodes from one podcast show per week. The show was still called Money Matters at this point. Around that time, a guest who came on the show said to me, "Adam, money matters, but mission matters, too." I immediately called my co-founder Chirag, and told him that Mission Matters is a great name. We looked at our content and realized that only about 20- percent of it was about money. We had outgrown the financial advisor brand and became bigger than the money management focus.

I sat on the idea for a couple of months while I continued to create content. Finally, Chirag called me and said, "Hey Adam, I've got this great idea. Let's call the company Mission Matters." I knew that creating a new website would be expensive, but we went for it. That's when we changed the name, and we have not looked back.

We partitioned the podcast content into eight different shows, which I still host today. Once again, I want to be clear, instead of boosting me as the influencer, we redirected those marketing dollars toward developing the Mission Matters Podcast Network. My journey to becoming a podcaster was a trial by fire, which turned out to be a blessing.

When you feel blessed, you want to bless others. Most people don't know how to create a podcast. I had to leave my financial services business to do this full time. We began to ask, how many other entrepreneurs and executives out there are going to take the time to figure out a podcast? Most either don't have the experience, or they're already successful, and don't have time to sit down and figure out production and distribution. It's not even on their radar. The problem with that is the best stories are not going to get told, so we felt it was that much more important to ensure our network was a place for those stories to be seen and heard..

Our mission for the Mission Matters Podcast Network is to bring on other entrepreneurs and executives who have a real story to share, or something they feel is a benefit to the world. We give them the chance to leverage our platform and have their voice amplified. Whether it's one person or a million people who are helped from their message, we also feel like we are helping people. That's the heart behind what we do. That heart has helped us build a network for many different entrepreneurs, business leaders and people who want to tell their stories.

As we continue to grow, we see that people come to us for many reasons. Some are interested in legacy, and they want to tell their story. Some want to grow their business and brand.

There were others who just wanted a digital footprint. If you Google people who are extremely accomplished, it is surprising that you find nothing online. They've done all these great things, but there's nothing to show their accomplishments . People want to be found online, even if it's only for reputation management. If they don't have anything out there, that's also a kind of reputation. There are very few vetted outlets to tell your story the way we do. In my opinion, it's hard to find a company you can trust to tell your story. Our clients want a vetted brand they can align with and trust.

Let me give you an example. An executive, who hosts a show on our network, was going for a big promotion. The person he was interviewing with looked him up online and he was able to say during the interview, "Yes, I have a podcast on this subject." That can be a very big deal. We are proud that we have such a variety of people on the network. We have executives. We have financial advisors. People use their podcasts for everything from business development to supporting a cause close to their heart. Helping each one of them with a platform to showcase whatever they need is an important part of our mission.

For me, success is helping someone tell their story so their message gets heard. One touching memory for me is about a client who had a book with us. We were having trouble contacting him. Eventually, his son got back to us and let us know he had passed. Surprisingly, his son didn't know his dad had a published book. Now, it's part of his legacy. His dad has a book on Amazon and he got to tell his story. He was an architect and his name and work will carry on with this book. It's also something his family can be proud of for years to come.

We had another client who transitioned out of the military, and decided to become an entrepreneur. She went into the armed forces when she was young and when she got out, she was a bit lost. The military is very regimented and also very different from civilian life. She had a hard time figuring out how the civilian world worked. She tells a story of standing in the cereal aisle at the grocery store, totally incapacitated by so many choices. It's amazing how something that small can be so tricky when transitioning to civilian life. That difficult moment inspired her to build an entire platform to help others make the same kind of transition.

She didn't plan to start a business. That wasn't her goal. But after going through our book process, she started to reevaluate what she wanted to do. In fact, when we first approached her, she had imposter syndrome. She didn't believe people would want to hear from her. Eventually, she understood she had a story that needed to be heard and a mission to share it with the world to help others. Now, she helps a lot of other people, which might not have happened if we hadn't brought her story out. She is one of our most meaningful success stories.

In fact, people began booking her for speaking engagements and other events, because she had a published book to showcase her story. Actually, that happens all the time to many of our authors. People view you differently when you have a published book. If you are a published author, you're likely to get booked as a speaker. That's just the way it works.

Another book I'm really proud of is our Women in Business Series. It was so enlightening to bring together an entire book full of women entrepreneurs, and to see some of their challenges. It's one thing to hear one of those stories, but to realize some of the similarities in their stories, it was eye-opening for me. Those similarities are interesting, because the authors don't talk to each other before the book is published. They don't know what anyone else is writing. And we don't tell them. For there to be an obvious theme across an entire book, from many women who are accomplished in many different industries, settings and career lengths, it was illuminating.

Another side of that story is how the women felt. Some were incredibly successful women who still struggled with imposter syndrome. They sometimes compared themselves to the guy who had less experience, but walked into a meeting confidently, talked confidently and suddenly everyone was listening to him, even though he was the least qualified person to make important decisions.

I act differently now, because of that book. I could see that's probably how I would have acted when I was in the finance world. I would have walked into a board room and said whatever I wanted to say. People would probably listen, if I seemed confident enough on whatever message I was delivering. There were definitely people in those rooms who were more qualified than me and probably had better insight. But, I had that personality. Those stories were very enlightening.

So many of the women's stories had similar examples, but in subtle ways. I would read a word and catch a feeling they were trying to convey, then I would see the same word in other women's stories. When I see similar themes emerge in our books, it lets me know how important this work is for those who choose to read it. I was inspired as a man reading these women's stories. And that's what inspires us to continue to build our platform.

Another book I consider to be a success is our Diversity Matters book. That one was very interesting. Not everyone in the book was an immigrant, but there were several people from various Asian cultures. To hear their experiences in corporate America, again from people who don't know each other, and to see those themes emerge, is interesting. Every story is different, but the whole book has deeply heartfelt stories, while still focusing around business leaders.I'm always excited to see what's going to come next with every book.

Looking back, I still feel the biggest challenge was the very first book. Getting our first book done was incredibly tricky. I had never published a book before, except the one for myself. We didn't have a model. We didn't know what the final book would look like. All we had was a deck for our company, describing an idea for entrepreneurs to come together into an anthology book series and a vision for what we thought it could be. We were aiming for a Chicken Soup for the Soul style of book, but focused more toward helping entrepreneurs and featuring entrepreneurs. That first book probably took us a solid year to produce, and it was difficult.

First, we didn't have anything we could show to clients. Then getting sign-offs for all of the chapters, without being able to show everyone a full manuscript, and having to manage and control the process of editing, became a full-time job. I also had to actually write some of it, which is something I had never done before. Plus, I was now responsible for 15 individual brands.

Then, I had to figure out the process to get it published. It was like trying to drive a car while it was being built. I didn't know anything about book publishing. I had to learn everything from understanding what a copyeditor does, to what a developmental editor does—yes, both have wildly different parts of the content they focus on. Every piece of knowledge, every challenge, every roadblock, every issue in publishing—we experienced it. We finished the project, but it was not easy. And after the book was done, then I had to figure out how to promote it.

This was when I began to see the parallels with my old skill-sets of being a financial advisor, and my utilization of systems and processes to complete work. I then had to figure out how to implement those in another style of business. As we built the first book, the system started to develop. We systematized everything from barcodes to copy to approvals, which made future books easier to produce and smoother to admin. We built out the entire model of what it would look like to deliver more books going into the future. We made tweaks along the way with each subsequent book, in order to make it a little better for the next one.

We did the same thing building the podcast agency. When I think back to my first interviews, I admit that it was crazy. I did between 70 and 80 interviews each week. They were in 15 to 20 minute interviews, and I worked from seven in the morning until seven at night, five or six days a week. We did that for a year, maybe more. I used to do an interview, then edit that interview, while I was doing the second interview. During the third interview, I did the distribution for the first interview. I kept that up throughout the day. Back then, when you did an interview with me, it would go live on multiple platforms within a couple hours.

That crazy interviewing, editing and distribution daily grind gave birth to our first strategic systems and processes. Once we started to get noticed, we were able to hire our first audio editor. At that time, we were audio only. I taught our editor the systems and processes, and fast forward to now—we've put out more than 40,000 pieces of content in the last five years. That would not have been possible without those strategic systems and processes.

I think some people approach systems the wrong way. They might think they need a grand plan in place for how they're going to scale their business. For Mission Matters, I started with me. I did the interviews. I edited them. I posted them. Over time, I got better at interviewing and better at editing. Then I was able to compress that time, because it became a skill.

I am sure my guests would see my posts on LinkedIn, and think, "Wait a minute, I just did an interview with this guy an hour ago. How is that even possible?" When I think about speed, service and reputation, I believe that was our product, our surprising ability that gave us a name in the industry. Of the millions of podcast shows being produced, I'd argue you will find very few that will have their podcast episodes edited and distributed across 40-plus platforms such as Spotify, Apple Podcasts and iHeart Radio, within a couple hours of the initial interview. That's what we did, and we did it really well, which got the attention of business leaders.

Many times, the person being interviewed wanted to know how we did it and how they could work with us. They didn't even care what we did. They would say, "What do you do? I want to work with you!" So many of them have bought a lot of marketing services from a lot of marketing companies. To them, what we did was like magic, and they loved the quality.

Based on the initial quality of content and reputation, we acquired clients with no advertising. We executed on what we said we would do, then exceeded expectations. I told them at the end of the interview that it would be out in the next five days. Then, they would see it in an hour. As we got bigger and more interviewees started to see the quality and exceeded expectations, then came all the crazy posts like, "I can't believe it. I just did this interview this morning and it's already up. This is unbelievable." We created raving fans, merely by producing a quality product using our systems and process that was far quicker than expected.

There are always different ways to look when solving a problem. Who would have thought that compressing the delivery time of someone's interview, while keeping the quality high, could have that much of an effect?

Someone might be out there thinking, my market is too crowded. I think anyone can come up with new ways to make a difference that may not even cost anything, except a little creative thinking about how to better serve a client. If you get creative enough, you could have people lining up to work with you, which is how all of our products evolved. Potential clients asked me how they could work with me, and I would say, "We're putting together a book. Do you want to be in a book?" I didn't think the people who I was interviewing would want to be in books, but they were impressed with what we were able to deliver. That's where it all started for us.

However, getting started and keeping that momentum going are two very different things. The media business is a tough game. It's hard. After 5,000 interviews, two things keep me in the game.

First, my dedication to the guest is a central focus of my process. I think Oprah explained this in an interview years ago. When you're interviewing people every day, and you have done it thousands of times, that's just your life. But for the person who is on the other side of the mic or in the book, this is a big moment for them. You have to be very purposeful with what you're doing, because it matters. The content will be out there for a long time, and you want to make sure they look good and have a great experience. And you want the audience to have a good experience, too.

Second, every story is new and different. It's a privilege knowing that you're helping someone tell their story and you're providing that moment when they feel connected to something bigger. Whether it's for acknowledgement for their career, or wanting to pass on information they think will be useful to others, it's that connection that they're striving for in their story, and it is our job to get it right for them.

Occasionally, there's an author or interviewee who might say something that sounds completely crazy to some people, but there will always be someone out there who hears it and thinks, this is my person. It may be exactly what someone needs to hear. There are a lot of unique people out there and I'm not here to judge. I want to help them get their story out there and feel connected. My advice to anyone who wants to do something new in business is to start and see where it takes you. Our journey to now at Mission Matters has been exciting, humbling, wild and the best adventure I've been on.

Chapter Six

Blows to the Side of the Head

– Elliot Kallen

"The greatest accomplishment is not in never falling, but in rising again after you fall."

~Vince Lombardi

Life is full of adversity. Schools teach us math, history and science. But they don't teach us how to handle adversity. Hardships, obstacles and challenges come in many forms, all of which can dramatically impact your life. Throughout history, the most preeminent leaders were those who took charge during times of crisis and managed to actualize victory.

In business, the late Steve Jobs was recalled to Apple when the company was facing a shrinking market share. His innovative approach to business made Apple the most profitable company in the world. In politics, no one has stood stronger in the face of adversity than Winston Churchill. If you're alive, you will have to deal with some form of adversity at some point in your life. The challenge is to stand strong in the face of that adversity.

In January 2015, my youngest son, Jake, took his life. That was a horrible experience that I don't wish on anybody, especially having to identify his body after being hit by a truck. But when the worst possible thing happens, we have to figure out a way to deal with it.

My son may have inherited depression from his mother, we don't know. In hindsight, we could see it coming during his senior year. He was a big man on campus, a hockey player extraordinaire with the Oakland Bears, both A and Travel Teams, and he had a car. I noticed when he would have a good game, he didn't seem excited or particularly happy. I would have been jumping out of my skin, but not Jake. After his death, parents told me that they noticed that Jake was withdrawn, even after scoring or having a great game. I asked them why they didn't share this with me at the time, but they were already upset with themselves for not sharing it with me.

We could see that he was doing very well in sports and activities, but he didn't seem to be enjoying himself, which we noticed, but missed some of the important clues of how much he was lost. My ex-wife and I talked about the fact that he wasn't enjoying life and something seemed off. I even asked her if she thought he might be depressed. We sat down with him and asked him if he was feeling sad or depressed. He would never admit to feeling bad, because that would mean he would be required to get some kind of help.

At Christmas, I decided to take everyone to Las Vegas to see some shows, eat some great food and have a good time. He said, "No, I just want to stay home by myself." I should never have let that happen. That was already a sign that he was beginning to withdraw from the family. But his mom said, "Just let him be. He's relaxing from school. Let him have some time off."

Jake was getting conflicting advice from his parents, which is not uncommon, and I will always feel bad about that. My ex-wife accused me of ruining the twins, by encouraging them to pursue business. She did not want that for Jake. I told him to follow his passions, which were sports and business. She wanted him to go into charity work. He had always been guilt-ridden about his mom's loneliness. He felt bad for her being alone and sad. It was an overwhelmingly powerful force in his life.

He liked big cats, so she encouraged him to major in wildlife biology. That summer, I helped him get an internship with a friend of mine in Montana, where he spent a lot of time alone. Looking back, that was a really bad idea. He told me later he really didn't like it that much, but he didn't want to tell his mom, which made him even more depressed. We visited him there and brought him home for part of the summer. Then, school started in the fall.

That October we had a family weekend, and I told him I would come up and buy some tickets to a Montana Grizzlies football game. We would have dinner, go to a home game and have some fun. We always had sports in common. We both loved the Jets, the Yankees and hockey. I was excited about spending time with him, but he put no effort into it. He didn't get the tickets or make reservations. I asked him why and he shrugged his shoulders like a dopey 19-year-old, and said, "I don't know."

I bought scalped tickets to the afternoon game and we went out to dinner at a local pub. I asked him how he was doing in classes, because I really got the feeling he was in the wrong major. He said he was okay with wildlife biology. I then asked how he was doing. He responded, "I'm dying." I didn't understand that he had stopped going to the science classes. No one reported that to me. When he told me he was dying, he meant that figuratively and literally. When he checked out, he created a path of failure for himself.

I told him he had to talk to his mom and tell her that he didn't want to be a wildlife biology major. I offered to do it for him, but he refused both options. The semester ended and he failed out of those two science classes, which he never told me. Unfortunately, we never talked about that subject again. One of my biggest regrets is that I didn't harp on his disengagement at school. When he came home from Christmas break, he wasn't the same. He wouldn't look me in the eye. While he was home, we went to a Sharks hockey game, but I could tell he wasn't enjoying it.

I had to do something, so I called his mom and told her something was wrong. Since she had suffered from depression, I asked if she would let him stay with her for two nights, so she could talk to him. She did. She thought I was overreacting and that he was just being a 19-year-old young man.

Later, at a party my wife and I threw, one of the adults told me, "Jake is turning into such a fine young man. He's so communicative." I thought, wow. Maybe it is just me.

Before Jake left for school in January, he couldn't look me in the eye. But he made a comment one day that gave me pause. He said, "You know, Dad, when I was in high school, I thought about suicide." I was cooking, so I stopped what I was doing and asked him how he was, feeling right then I asked if he was thinking about it and if he wanted to get some help. I told him we could talk about it. He said, "No, that's come and gone." But it hadn't.

He said something different to his mom. He said, "You know, Mom, when I'm gone, you're going to miss me." I didn't know about that until later, but if you put those two things together, he was talking about suicide in his own way. That's why we talk about communication triggers on our website, *www.ABrighterDay.info*. Those types of conversations are triggers.

When he left for school, he turned his head away and could not look me in the eyes to say goodbye. His mom took him to the airport, but I told my wife that something was wrong. I could feel it in my gut. I called my ex-wife a few days later, and said, "I'm going up to Montana. I want to meet with Jake. Something is very wrong." She thought I was overreacting and I should give him a few more weeks.

By the middle of the next week, I realized I'd never seen any grades from the previous semester. I left a message for Jake, but got no reply. I called the school to ask for his grades. They told me they were not allowed to give me his grades, but because I had a good relationship with the people there, they told me anyway. He got a D-minus in both of those science classes. I was informed that he could get a C just by showing up, so I knew he stopped going to class.

I called and left a strong and direct voicemail for Jake, and even sent an email as a follow-up to the voicemail. I thought tough love was the answer and I knew something was wrong. I told him that I knew about the two science classes, and that we needed to have a conversation about why he was there. I also said that we needed to maybe address changing majors, and possibly coming back to a junior college back home to regroup. I even suggested that maybe school was not for him and that he could get a job. Or, if he wanted, I could use my contacts to get him into the Air Force. However, I got no response.

We finally spoke on a Tuesday. I was mad at him, and I wanted to find a way to make things better between us. I said, "Jake, this summer, I'm going to take everyone to Israel for a couple of weeks. It will be kind of an early reward for graduation. I know you're working on stuff. Don't worry about it. We'll go, clear our heads and we'll get through this." He told me that the trip sounded great. However, I believe he had already written his suicide note by then.

I called his mother again and said I was going up there that weekend. I also told her that something was really wrong. She tried hard to talk me out of it, by saying I was overreacting again and putting too much pressure on him. That was Wednesday night. On Thursday night, around 9 p.m., his mother called me very upset. She told me Jake made a bad comment that day. He said, "Mom, I'm at peace now." I think, by the time he called her, he had already sent his suicide note by FedEx. He said goodbye to his mom. He didn't say goodbye to me. From what we know or the information we have received since, that night after he called his mom, he turned his phone off and made his bed. He forgot to turn off his computer. When we opened it, it opened to a page describing the best ways to commit suicide. His clothes were all put away, but he had not unpacked his Hanukkah gifts. He walked or jogged up to the highway, waited for a truck to come by and jumped in front of the truck at around 1:45 a.m. There were no drugs or alcohol in his system.

All day Friday, both his mother and I were calling and leaving messages, because we were both on the same page that something was wrong and we needed to do anything we could to help him. Because he had no ID on him, he was in the morgue as a John Doe. Around 6:30 p.m. that night, FedEx delivered an envelope with his suicide note. Panic set in immediately. We both began what would be the hardest hours of our life until then, not knowing what happened to our son.

I told his mom to call the hospitals and I called the campus police to get to his dorm. They say they couldn't go knocking on dorm rooms. The hospital said, "Mrs. Kallen, hang up the phone. The sheriff is going to call you right back." A minute later, they called and told her our son was dead and that he had jumped in front of a truck.

She called me hysterical. I said, "I need you to keep it together for a moment." She asked me why. I responded, "Because we have to go get his body. If you don't want to do it, I'll do it myself." She said, "I read the suicide note. He wants to be cremated and have his ashes spread in the Montana mountains." I made a decision on the fly. I told her that I didn't owe that to him anymore. I owed this to the living. I made the decision to bring him back. We are Jewish and I wanted to have a burial and a funeral.

Many people immediately began to help me. As we flew up to Montana, I kept reading the suicide note. On the way to the morgue, we were pulled over by the police. I swerved and went right through a stop sign, next to where people were building a little memorial to Jake. I apologized to the officer and explained that the kids were creating the memorial for my son. He asked where I was going, and I said, "To the morgue." He let me go.

When we got to the morgue, they warned us not to touch the body, because he had basically been crushed. I already spoke to them on the phone, so I knew what they would say about the circumstances of his death. Due to us wanting the Jewish funeral, they couldn't embalm him. So, they put him on dry ice. They told me they had just put his face back together, put a mouth guard in his mouth and glued it shut. However, he had no eyes, because they took them out to donate the retinas.

Even though I heard what they said and knew they didn't want me to touch him, of course, you can't tell a parent not to touch their dead son. I touched him, and there was nothing there below the neck. It was devastating. I called other family members in to see him if they wanted to. His mom was screaming, and said, "I'm Jewish. I need his body parts." The coroner just said, "They're all there. They're just crushed, and flat and broken in so many places."

After we left the morgue, we went back to the hotel where I had my room and his mom had her room. I couldn't sleep. At about 11 p.m., my wife called, who had stayed back home, and we talked until 7 a.m. The next morning, we went over to the school where they had a hockey memorial to honor Jake and his life. The coach decided to retire his jersey, because Jake set so many records for scoring goals. We wanted to head home instead of going to the event, but couldn't get a plane out that day anyway, because Montana has laws against flying bodies on weekends, so we went to the rink. There were a couple of TV stations there, as well as radio stations. I did some interviews and tried to hold it together the best I could. There were 300 people in the stands, because hockey is a big deal in Montana. The coach called close to 50 players out onto the ice. They all took off their helmets and gloves, and then laid their sticks on the ice, as they raised Jake's jersey to the rafters where it will stay forever. It was a very sad day.

During the memorial, the coach spoke highly of Jake. He said, "He was a good kid. I should have known better, because he was isolating himself in the locker room. I just thought it was a quirk of personality. I didn't realize he was withdrawing. I'm a hockey coach with a PhD in anatomy and I didn't know that. So, there's no blame here for anybody." He also talked about Jake's friends and while he spoke, people were openly crying.

Then the coach went on to say, "I'd like everybody to do something for me. I'd like you to put your hand on your wrist and feel your pulse." People did that. Then he said, "I'd like you to put your hand over your mouth and feel the temperature of your breath. These are the two signs you're alive. Never forget to stay alive. There are two parents in the crowd crying, because somebody forgot to stay alive." That's still hard to say. There was a photo of it on the front page of the Montana newspaper.

On the way home, we got on the plane and watched the metal travel casket get loaded underneath us. When we got to Vegas for the plane change, I didn't see the casket get loaded. I called the flight attendant over and explained, "I can't leave, unless I'm sure my son's body is on this plane." She gave me a shocked look, then came back moments later to say that the captain would personally check, which he did.

The funeral home was wonderful when we set everything up for Jake. There's no open casket at a Jewish funeral, but we wanted the family to come and say goodbye to him one last time. There was only so much they could do to prepare the body, but they did a great job. The ride home after the funeral was obviously very quiet. I kept reading the suicide note over and over. Four of the six pages were rambling, but that first paragraph said, "Mom, Dad, I've been thinking about this for a long time. I never would have asked for help. I never would have taken your help. And I never would have told you how I felt."

That stuck with me. He went on to say, "Don't blame the truck driver, don't blame Montana. It wasn't the school. It wasn't my friends. It was my decision, mine alone." But he also said several times, "Mom, I hope you can find happiness one day." The only thing he directed to me was, "Dad, I knew you were always doing your best with me."

I remember when we were on the plane home from Montana, I told my ex-wife that we were always going to be victims of this and that we needed to help other parents so they don't become victims of this as well. That was my thought process; that's how I chose to focus my grief. I've always thought that you have to establish a path to success. I wasn't articulating it very well at that time, but that's what I was saying. I didn't want to be wallowing in this forever.

I believe experiencing your child's mortality is the greatest adversity you could ever face. It was important to me to come up with some positive tribute from that horrible malaise.

When I returned to work about a week later, I would sit in my chair. I put my goals and my vision away and tried to work, but then I would see his picture and start crying. I couldn't think. It was a good two or three months before I could take phone calls again, or even think about what I was doing.

That's when I began the work of starting the charity nonprofit. I articulated goals for the charity to people over and over again, which helped me get codified in my mind. I wanted to run toward success and make a difference in the lives of people who might be facing similar circumstances. Everyone makes a difference to someone else around them, because everyone touches others all the time. We benefit each other in business and in our personal lives. The question is, can you keep doing that, or are you going to be too busy in your own world?

As I progressed through my grief, our charity, *A Brighter Day,* was formed. We created a massive amount of resources for depression and suicide. Then, we needed to figure out how to get them into the hands of people who needed them. My first thought was to have a sports-oriented charity. We would go to sporting events and set up a table, where teenagers could pick up pamphlets with valuable information regarding suicide prevention and ways to talk about their depression. But I quickly learned that a lot of teenagers no longer do sports. So, we became music-centered instead.

At the time, I thought I would become a music promoter. Somehow, I'd find a way to make these concerts free so teens would come to them. I met with several cover bands who I knew personally and they all said I was doing it the wrong way. There should be teens playing for teens, and we shouldn't have a table set up, because they will never go over to that table in front of their friends. I was told we have to put them in their hands. That's how we came up with the concept of giving out string backpacks, filled with resources on stress and depression. We handed them out during the concerts.

We had 1,000 teens come to concerts our first year. We knew parents were reading our resources, because they were sending us notes and saying thank you for giving this to their teen. The materials were not judging the teens for how they feel, they encouraged them to get help. They also encouraged parents to get help, to start talking to their child and gave them resources on how to ask their teen if they were feeling sad or depressed, or if they had thoughts of suicide.

Today, we have touched thousands of families. Last year, 14,000 people touched our resources in some form. Last month, it was almost 10,000. It's growing exponentially and we are making a difference.

Since the onset of the COVID-19 pandemic, we have had to change our approach again. We focused on talent, instead of concerts, but it's still a music-based charity. We have become more of a resource for parents, because we realize it is easier to get to teens through their parents, than through other teens. We have created a texting program for teens and parents, where they can text and get help within five minutes. Anyone 13 years old or older can get a 40-minute call, as many times as they need. We also created a Zoom counseling session, where the first one is free, with ongoing paid support available for both teens and parents. They can go straight to their computer or their cell phone, 24 hours a day. The goal is to prevent teens from committing suicide, and prevent parents from having to feel the devastation we felt losing our son Jake. That's the motivation behind the charity.

My advice to any teen who is struggling is to get help in some way. Jake kept this from us, which is not healthy, but it is very common. For a parent, I would ask them to do whatever they can to open up the lines of communication with their teen. I'm talking about in-depth conversations, not just asking them what they are up to. I know everyone's busy working and shuffling kids to events. But try to take time, especially at dinner. Make it a cell phone free time and open up conversation. And when you realize you have uncovered something, talk about getting help. You need help to deal with the situation, because you won't know what questions to ask.

We help with creating healthy conversations by sending emails to parents with good questions to ask their teens. It's important to ask them about themselves. Ask about their best classes and worst classes. And ask about their friends. Sometimes, teens won't talk about themselves, but they will talk about their friends. If you'd like more information, check out our website at *ABrighterDay.info.*

While helping others can be a welcome distraction from your own pain and suffering, as a parent who has lost a child, I have realized that you still need to make sure you help yourself. I never got self-destructive when my son died, or when I was going through my divorce. Of course I do know that not following goals is a form of self-destruction. You don't have to take drugs or get drunk to be self-destructive. You can also be in a world of inaction. Those types of emotional strains can create inaction and victimhood.

Having a vision is not only for the good times. Having a vision born out of adversity can be even more powerful than one born out of dreams and wishes. I always thought my life's legacy would be about helping people have a better retirement. I want to leave them with a better way of life and an opportunity to reach their goals, travel and hand money down to their children. And that part is hopefully still true. But at the end of the day, I think my real legacy is changing the lives of parents and teens. But how do I measure that?

Theoretically and biblically, if you change one person, you've done a good job. But we are changing hundreds of lives and hopefully one day, we will be changing thousands of lives. And not because it's a gateway to heaven, but because it's the right thing to do. And, I don't want anyone to go through what I went through.

Doing good is always a winning strategy. You don't have to start a charity to make a difference. You could drop in and help out at a homeless shelter. As children, my mother made us shovel snow for Mrs. Williams, who was 80. We hated it, but now I understand why my mother made us do it. My dad wasn't a big giver of money, but he gave his time and shared his family to help others. That was his charity.

There are so many people who are less fortunate and could use a hand. It's amazing how fortunate we all are, no matter how unfortunate we feel our circumstances are. The poorest of Americans are richer than some of the middle class of the poorest countries. Whether you're cooking turkeys at Glide Memorial Church on Thanksgiving, or you want to volunteer and be part of something bigger than you, it feels good to do good. And doing good can be an important part of healing your own adversity.

If you would like more information about A Brighter Day, please check out the Appendix at the end of the book. It has valuable tools and resources for parents, teens and organizations. Or you can visit the website, *ABrighterDay.info*.

CHAPTER SEVEN

COMMUNITY DOESN'T JUST HAPPEN

– ELLIOT KALLEN

"Success is empty if you arrive at the finish line alone. The best reward is to get there surrounded by winners."

~Howard Schultz

The world is bigger than you. The younger generations today often behave as if they are the center of the universe. When I was growing up, I was taught we are all cogs in the wheel of life. In today's "me" world, people believe they are the wheels of life.

People tend to be in two different camps on this. People who are 55 and older come from my kind of world. My generation and the generation before me are the biggest donors on the planet. We give to causes. We start charities and foundations. The generation from 21 to 35 give the least. If it doesn't affect them, they don't seem to care. It's one of the reasons attendance at churches and synagogues are down 40- to 60-percent across the board in this country. From the "me" point of view, who cares? They don't know if they believe in God, and they think their character is just fine.

It's really not about believing in God. It's about believing in something bigger than yourself. Whether it's God, community or family doesn't matter. I have always lived my life with charity. Give. And think bigger than you. There are so many people in need.

I started my charity, *A Brighter Day,* in my mind, 48-hours after my son died. I was already thinking about how it would work. I knew I had to give back, because I strongly believe we have to help other people. I knew we weren't the only ones going through this. Yes, we were victims, but I wanted to stop other people from becoming victims. In my grieving state, I didn't know the how or the when yet, but I knew at that time, we were going to start the charity.

I used to be president of the Boys and Girls Club. I was part of the American Cancer Society. I was involved with the local Jewish Community Center. Even in college, I was a student advisor to one of the adult boards. That was important to my family, because they knew I would go to the meetings and learn not to be so shy. I believe when you give, you often receive both tangible and intangible gifts in return. However, that's not why you do it.

Community is community, whether it's inside your company, your family, your city or your religious community. You are part of a community, and you can choose to be a pillar of that community, because community members trust you and believe in you. They believe in you, because of what you've done, not who you are. Sometimes, they love who you are, but not what you've done.

I've been fortunate enough to have some success. I've always given back at least 10-percent of my income, plus an enormous amount of time. Again, it's about the tangible and intangible gifts you can provide the world. When I was president of my synagogue, it was a 30-hour per week job, in addition to my regular work. My son died while I was president, but I stayed true to what I was doing and continued to serve as well as work, because I felt both were bigger than me.

Starting a foundation makes the problem you are personally facing bigger than your pain. Helping other people reach their dreams is also bigger than you. You cannot be a great financial advisor if it's about you and your paycheck. It has to be about helping others reach their goals. My clients are bigger than me. I always ask what's important to them in their retirement? They waited their entire life to spend time with their grandchildren. They waited their whole life to take a really great vacation. I want to help them reach those goals and together I believe we can do it. I want to make this about them, not me, and help them reach their goals. That's community. That's what makes someone good in my business—helping others reach their goals, not your personal or business goals.

I think a good community person is a selfless person. They think about how they fit in and how they can help before saying, what about me?

I believe the Lone Wolf model of entrepreneurship is a problem. The Lone Wolf doesn't care. It's one of the reasons Elon Musk has a high turnover at his plants. He is not a consensus builder. He's very different from Steve Jobs and his management skills. No one, in the history of any and all products, has ever done a better job of building consensus and loyalty than Steve Jobs. I don't know any more loyal fans or employees to a brand and company than Apple. And he was a terrible person to work with, but people had so much respect for him and they loved him.

If you are out there trying to be the Lone Wolf, learn how to build consensus instead. Learn how to get people to buy into you, versus making them do what you want. We live in a different world than we did a decade ago. Even though there's a recession going on, people can get a job if they really want one. Which means, my staff could walk out the door tomorrow. But if they buy into what I'm doing, and I reward them, thank them and become a part of their lives, it's more than merely business. I care about the people in my business. If you don't care, no one wants to be around you.

In my office, we do friendly things. We have wine outings all the time. We do dinners. I buy lunches, because we want to be together, not because I want people eating at their desks. We are team people.

Your community is made up of people, and people are your most important resource, as well as the thing you need to protect and support most.

When I moved to California, I knew two people. That was it. I immediately joined a synagogue to meet people. I joined LeTip, which is a networking group like Business Network International (BNI). I grabbed the Jewish newspaper every week to see which companies took out ads. I called them up and asked if I could network with them. Most of them said no. But some said yes. I waited for the yeses.

I did dialing for dollars when I first started, but I don't wish that on anyone. I was making so little money back then, I could have gone to McDonald's and gotten a raise. I actually took a second job at night selling gym memberships, which was also a terrible job. Eventually, I started to develop my business and make enough money at Lincoln Financial to quit my gym job.

The financial industry can be incredibly product-centered. They want all 500 branches in the United States to sell AT&T stock ... today. That is the opposite of what I think is right for my clients. I'm not interested in selling you the stock someone else is pumping.

The business model at Lincoln was sales. They wanted you to sell a product today. It was not about building long-term clients. That was not the place for me, because I wanted to be people-focused, not product-centered. I'm interested in doing the right thing for my community, in an industry that doesn't always do that. Some people call that character. I call it me.

CHAPTER EIGHT

CHARACTER COUNTS

– ELLIOT KALLEN

"Challenges are gifts that force us to search for a new center of gravity. Don't fight them. Just find a new way to stand."

~Oprah Winfrey

For any entrepreneur who has gone through a recession or a divorce, both of those create gigantic headwinds in your life, because they can be out of your control. During a recession, everything starts slowing down around you, while you're still going the same speed. You begin looking around and asking yourself, what's going on?

As an entrepreneur, you have to think differently when there's a recession, versus a bull market in front of you, which means stocks and prices rise and investors are optimistic. That means, cash becomes king. And every decision needs to be a smart decision, because a poor decision could cost you your entire opportunity.

When the recession hit in 2001, at the same time as my divorce, I remember making a conscious decision—I was not going to fail. That meant I had to do everything in my power to succeed. The need to succeed was my motivation when everything was falling down around me. I kept plowing through. As I write this in 2023, I see a similarly tough financial time coming toward us.

My advice is you have to plow through a recession, because you will lose clients, and you will lose friends. A lot of negative things happen during recessions, because stress levels go way up. In my business, people lose money. While I know it has nothing to do with me, it is still my job to help my clients with their finances the best I can. I have nowhere to put your money, except maybe a savings account, which is six points below inflation and that means you are also losing money. There's nowhere to hide.

Those two motivators, the drive to succeed and the fear of failure, are the yin and yang of being an entrepreneur. They are a constant battle. Then, there's that little devil on your shoulder who says, "If only I had a shortcut, I could succeed faster." Those thoughts make you think about where you could cut corners to do better. The recession shakes out people who cut corners. Suddenly, they're on the edge of what's legal and ethical.

Your ethical metal gets tested when times get tough. But that's also your opportunity to strengthen and show fortitude from within. Your character gets tested in tough times, not in good times. Good times rarely test your character. I guess people in the 1980s had so much free money, they ended up doing cocaine all day. That was the test of the 80s. When times are good, you don't need to take a shortcut, because everything is good. But in tough times, you want to take a shortcut, because it's tough. This is when your ethics are always in question. Entrepreneurs who have defined ethics, depending on how rigid they are, tend to fare better. But for people who have undefined ethics, they tend to go with the flow. That's what gets you into trouble.

I have found in business, for certain people, and certain immigrant groups especially, bribes are standard practice. I can remember when I wanted to sell a group medical plan or a group 401k, I was asked to kick back some of the money I was making to the HR manager or the CFO. I knew that was unethical and I could lose my license for doing it. Maybe, if I wasn't going to lose my license, I might have thought differently. But I knew I was being tested. I knew I would lose my license if it ever got reported, so I had to walk away from that business, knowing someone else would be willing to pay the bribe.

This happened with one of my largest clients. We were about six months into the relationship, when he said, "I'm going to need you to give half of what you make back to me and my boss." He wanted the money to continue working with us. It was very sad. I had to let it go. I even came back to my office and thought about it. Do I do this? However, in the end, I said no. I cannot say this any other way … you don't do this, no matter what. I immediately lost him as a client. To this day, I still cross paths with the owner of that company, and I have never told him what happened. Even though his people were unethical, I don't throw anyone under the bus. I kept it to myself and moved on. It was a 100-percent cultural thing. Thankfully, in America, we don't live in a world where you have to bribe your way to success. However, in other cultures, they do.

There was a very funny movie from 1990 called *The Freshman*, with Marlon Brando, who played a New Your City Mafioso-type named Carmine Sabatini, and Mathew Broderick, who played Clark—an unsuspecting college student from Vermont, who ended up working for the Marlon Brando character. At one point in the film, Clark tried to figure out if he could trust Carmine and he asked, "You promise?" The Marlon Brando character said in his best Godfather voice, "Every word I say, by definition, is a promise." I feel the same way. Your words should convey strength and character.

When I was young, my dad would constantly tell me everything I say must be true. You must follow through. You can't stand people up. You can't flake out. You can't invite people, and then uninvite them. That's not how things work. Your word must be your bond. Your word has to be gold. It's more important than your handshake or any contract you will ever sign. A contract is only as good as the person who signs it. This is so important in any field.

In business and in my world, anytime we said we were going to do something, we did it. If something comes up, we don't let it go. We don't hide from it. We get out in front of it. For some people, their world is all about "me." My mom and dad were all about the "we." Focusing on "we" over "me" was about character for them.

In the "we" world, you live in a community of strength, and of friends, where you are a part of something much bigger than yourself. Whatever you call it, community begins with charity. And this means you need to learn to give of yourself to other people. It doesn't mean you can write a check and feel good about saving the whales. It really is about giving of yourself.

When I was a kid, we had an older cousin who owned a bicycle store. He couldn't afford to hire extra help, so my dad would drop us off and we helped him build bicycles on Saturdays. Our only pay was a hamburger and fries for lunch, because, as my dad would say, you give your gift to people in need. On Thanksgiving, we would go from nine in the morning until noon and serve food to people who couldn't afford to buy it. It's something we've always done as a family and it has spilled over into my business.

When my kids played hockey, there was a homeless guy named Eddie, who hung around outside the ice rink and asked us for money all the time. One day, I said to Eddie, "I don't mind giving you a dollar here or there, but you need to do something for the money." He asked what I would suggest he do. I said, "Wash my car. Wash my windows. Something that says you've earned it. I'll give you much more money if you do that."

We brought him window cleaner and rags. Every time I went there, three days a week, I had the cleanest wheels and the cleanest windshield. We made Eddie work for his money and he felt like he was accomplishing something. Suddenly, he was buying his own window cleaner and rags, and he provided a service to make a little bit of money. My kids and I talked about this and it was one of those life lessons about hard work, being non-judgmental of other people, and making sure your character always counts. Your word is your bond is a reflection of your character.

When I was about 10, my dad owned an ink and supply business. He sold ink and solvents directly into shipping rooms and factories in the 1960s, back when no one had security systems in place. You could walk right in. I remember the ballgame would be on the TV, because the Yankees and the Mets played during the day back then. No one would steal anything. It wasn't like today, when things are stolen and there are cameras in every direction. There was a trust back then.

My dad brought me into his company one day. I was 10 years old, sporting a little bow tie. He introduced me to Ernie, the Black gentleman who ran the shipping department. I stuck out my hand and shook his. Even though this was the 1960s, he was Black and I was white, I didn't really think twice about it. When we got into the car, my dad asked, "What did you think about Ernie?" I grumbled like any 10-year-old would, and said, "He seems nice." Then my dad asked, "What did you think of him being Black?" I was a little dumbfounded by the question and replied, "I don't know." My dad asked, "Then why did you look at your hand after you shook his hand?" I had not noticed I did it and told my dad so. He responded, "You did. Did you think the color was going to rub off?"

I was embarrassed and felt bad about it. My dad went on to say, "When you shake someone's hand, you never judge people on color. And you never judge them on title. There are CEOs who are horrible people, and there are janitors and shipping room people who are some of the best people you will ever meet on earth. Make sure that when you choose your friends, you don't choose them for their income, title, religion or race. Choose them by who they are."

I have always been the guy who has had friends of all races and religions. I don't care about any of that. I choose people, because of who they are. I see the exact opposite in people who proudly announce they surround themselves with all these great CEOs, because that's how they judge themselves. I have a friend who is worth about $100 million dollars. He calls himself the poorest of his friends, because he only hangs out with people who are close to being billionaires. That's how he judges you. He actually told me he only wanted to go out with me once a year, because he didn't want people to see him with me. "It will say something about me, because you're not in my net worth," he explained. That's a pretty hard way to make or keep a friendship.

My business is the world of money, so of course I'd love to hang out with billionaires, because they can give me big checks to invest. But from a character standpoint, some of them are the biggest jerks. They're often drunks and lack moral character. They do many things right, but they are far from perfect. Lately, when we elect our officials, character seems to have no value. People hold their nose and vote.

I also understand we don't live in a black and white world. It's not a perfect world. I consider it more of a gray world. If you try to live in a black and white world, you're going to get your nose bloodied all the time. If you live in a gray world, where you understand where someone else is coming from, then it helps where you're coming from as well. Sometimes, we are so focused on what we want to say, we forget about how it's being heard. Just listen. Then, formulate your response.

There are many great qualities of good character. Honesty, integrity and your word being your bond is a starting point for anyone who wants to build a life of value. I also believe having a great sense of humor should be on this list. It's highly underrated. And I'm not talking about the guy at the comedy club. I'm talking about being funny and having fun.

When I got divorced 20 years ago, several of my friends suggested I date women who were 25 years old. And when they turned 30, I should break up with them. Their reasoning was, I had the energy of a 25-year-old. My energy levels are high and I sleep little. I thought about that for a very brief period of time. Minutes. It didn't sink in though.

I quickly realized I wanted to be with someone I could have a great conversation with and laugh at life experiences. I wanted us to make fun of ourselves and make fun of each other. My wife, Tammy, makes fun of me all the time. She was able to talk my kids into making fun of me as well. They always gang up on me. When Tammy's son came to live with us, he joined in, too. Everybody instigates each other against me, and that's okay, because it's fun, and easy to do. It's important to have a good sense of humor and to have fun with each other.

I'm not the class clown, but I did irritate a few teachers in my day. I enjoy playing off what other people say, and I like to laugh and have fun. One day, a friend told me I should do stand up. I memorized about 17 jokes and got on stage at a comedy club back east, during Open Mic Night. As soon as I stepped on stage, my brain went blank. I just stood there. I rolled my eyes back into my brain, hoping I'd see something. I didn't see anything. It was a humbling experience. The audience was incredibly patient with me. I think they all felt my pain at that moment.

I learned something about myself that night. I'm a quipper. I'm good at improvisation. I need you to say something, so I can then build on it. There were three comedians that night. The first guy was really working the audience. He was asking people questions and playing off whatever they said. I need that to happen for me to be funny. Just standing there, and saying, "Two guys walk into a bar with an alligator …," is not me. People who know me say, "He's great in a crowd," because that's what I do. I also don't take myself too seriously. I can make fun of myself all day and not feel threatened.

This is what I do in meetings. Someone will say something and I build on it. I might say something clever, like I actually know what I'm talking about. But I'm just as likely to say something ridiculously silly. Sometimes it works well, and sometimes it falls flat.

I try to be witty. I'm quipping all day. Making fun of yourself is very disarming. But beware: Self-deprecation is different. People don't want to be around people who are constantly self-deprecating. I can make fun of myself being only five-foot-eight. I joke that I peaked at five-foot-nine, but now I'm five-eight, at least in the morning. That's making fun of myself.

Lots of people are taller than me. I do business with people who are six-foot-four, six-foot-five, and six-foot-six. They have to bend down to give me a hug. And some of them are women. I tease them, saying, "I hate you bending down to give me a hug, because it makes me feel short." They say they don't mind, because they want to make me feel better. And I reply, "I guess it's better than being five-foot-two. My dad was five-foot-two and my mom was only five feet tall. I'm six inches taller and a hundred pounds heavier than my dad was. I'm a giant in my family."

Last night, we were Zooming with my brother who is six feet tall. My wife asked him, "Norm, how much do you weigh?" He responded that he weighs 155 pounds. My wife turned to me and said, "Do you realize you weigh 50 pounds more than your brother?" I told her that I got it. Of course, that became a big joke. I was heavier than him when he was in the eleventh grade and I was in seventh grade.

The point of all that fun is we are never attacking anyone's character with our humor. It's about being able to lighten up, not weighing everyone down. Yes, pun intended. If you are the one who sets the tone for being light, it's disarming for everyone around you, especially the most important people in your life.

It's a big trait of mine as a business owner. My staff members feel welcomed around me. They can walk into my office, sit down, and say, "Can we talk? I have this issue going on." Or, "This is really bothering me." Or, "Did you know you said this to me?"

One of the hazards of always being humorous and trying to have fun is it can occasionally land on someone who is not in the mood. Maybe you're having a bad hair day, and I say, "Did you brush your hair today?" I was trying to be witty, but it caught you at the wrong moment. I might not even know you're upset. At some point, I have to realize I've upset you and deal with it. I have to apologize and hopefully, find something witty about that.

Another thing that reveals character is how you overcome obstacles. If you're an entrepreneur, obstacles are going to be thrown at you all the time. There are several obstacles you will invariably have to deal with at any given time. These are not in any particular order, however, they are things that happen.

Health Challenges. There are so many great stories about people who have overcome health challenges, like cancer or diabetes or heart disease. One of the classic stories is of Col. Sanders. He had heart disease and other challenges at

65 years old from a lifetime of eating too many fried foods. He tried to sell his special recipe. People liked it, but they didn't want to pay him for it. Instead, he opened his own restaurant and later franchised it. At 73, he became overwhelmed with his health and running the company, so he sold it and became a paid brand ambassador for Kentucky Fried Chicken.

Almost every entrepreneur experiences some sort of health challenge, either their own, their spouse's or a family member's, which they have to overcome. An entrepreneur's world is filled with setbacks, but they are not the end of things. Being an entrepreneur is kind of like running one of those mud races with obstacles. You're constantly jumping over things, going under other things and getting yourself muddy. You may get a bloody nose, but you pick yourself up, dust yourself off, put on clean clothes and get back out there. If you're starting a business from scratch, you might be sleeping in the office or in your car in the beginning to try to keep the business in the green. However, whatever you're doing, you need to take care of your health.

Divorce. Divorce is higher among entrepreneurs than the average person, because the entrepreneur is not only married to his or her spouse, they're also married to their business. It's their work-spouse, or worse, their baby. They live and die with it. They're up in the middle of the night, thinking about cash flow. They're hiring and firing. There are people who are close to you who you need to get rid of and positions you need to fill. Unfortunately, your marriage can often come last.

When I was married to my first wife, I always felt like family was the most important thing. And I still believe that today. When I left Lincoln Financial, started Prosperity Financial Group, and got divorced all at the same time, my first thought was, why bother working at all? I was so sad. I felt like my world was torn out from under me. With three little babies at five and four years old, I felt like I screwed up my children. I would come to work and stare at my screen. A lot of people in similar situations bleed their emotions all over everybody and call it a day. They don't really do anything positive. They self-destruct.

I didn't want to be like other people who couldn't stop talking about what a horrible spouse or soon-to-be ex-spouse I had. I kept saying I wanted her to be happy. But in reality, I was miserable wanting her to be happy. Unfortunately, you have to go through it.

The reality is divorce is a death. It's the death of a marriage. Whether you caused it or the other person caused it, or it's a star that burned out, it's still sad.

I had my kids four and a half days out of seven, every week. When I didn't have them, I would run to the gym early in the morning and play racquetball to beat myself up. When I didn't have the kids, I also would play hockey late at night. Sometimes, I finished playing and got home at 12:30 in the morning. Because I was a goalie, I allowed myself to get pounded that much more. I was beating myself up at the gym in the morning, followed by beating myself up at work and feeling sorry for myself, followed by beating myself up until late at night playing hockey.

I was not letting myself heal or move through the pain. I would only allow myself to get beat up four days a week. The other days were torture, because I emotionally bled at work and had to find a way to take care of the kids without letting them see my pain. I finally started to turn around my mindset by coaching myself and telling myself I could do this; I had a right to be happy; I had a right to be successful. That's what has to happen when you're facing an obstacle of any force. Your force has to be equal to or greater than the opposite force, which includes the force of your mindset.

A good entrepreneur understands challenges are just obstacles they have to overcome. For me, it took a while. It was definitely not overnight. It took about a year and a half to get up and say, "I can do this. I'm worthy of earning good money and I'm a creative, fun guy. I can do this again."

Divorce and health and death are more walls you have to climb. Health has its own problems. When you're facing a serious health issue, you need to have the will and the power to get out of it.

I also started to watch a lot of comedy movies. I watched copious amounts of Abbott and Costello. I knew if I could laugh at those guys, I could also begin to laugh at myself again. I wanted to be the funny guy again. Laughing at yourself is getting a head start on your competition, because they're going to laugh at you anyway. Your family is still going to laugh at you, because you're basically the same little kid who put your pants on the wrong way and was once in a diaper.

Loss of a Loved One. The hardest obstacle of all to deal with is the loss of a loved one. For many, it's the loss of a parent. For me, it was the loss of a child. These are major setbacks. With the loss of a parent, at least you can justify they were older and lived a full life. But, some people can't get over losing their parents. Losing a spouse is a horrible situation to have to face. And losing a child, there's always going to be a hole in your heart. My son's picture is my screensaver. Pretty hard to get around that.

What I eventually realized—and it took me a while to get to this place—was life moves on. Tomorrow, the sun will come up and the world will keep spinning. People are going to succeed, with or without me. My company is going to move forward, with or without me. It might as well move forward with me.

I recognized I am part of something bigger than myself. And rather than wallow in my sorrow, which is a very easy thing to do, even today, I realize I am one of many cogs in the wheel. And I need to make the best of whatever situation I'm in. That's why I started a 501(c)(3) non-profit charity, to make the best of the situation, and in this case, a very ugly situation.

Previous Business Failures. Another obstacle to overcome is previous business failures. Not all entrepreneurs succeed on their first venture. Col. Sanders pushed through a lot of problems. Harry Truman went bankrupt in the haberdashery business, before going on to become president. Abraham Lincoln had many failures in his life. Richard Branson's first business failed. There are people who have lots of business failures.

Business failures and business learning experiences are integrally connected with each other. Everyone has failures on a daily basis. Life is filled with failures.

But for entrepreneurs, I don't believe you have a failure, until you admit it was a failure. It's a learning lesson. It didn't go well. What can I do better? What if I did this differently?

The number one cause of business failures is running out of cash. People misdirect their cash flow. Another is trying to do something that's not your core competency, or getting distracted. There's nothing wrong with having a business failure. You're only down when you stay down. So, get up. Mike Tyson once said, "Everybody has a plan, until they get punched in the mouth."

Looking back at the failure of my first business, I would call it an immature, novice business failure. My cash flow was out of control, and when I tried to raise money, the cost of it was too high. Instead, I sold the assets and kept the liabilities, which I paid off over the next few years. Even though I made everyone whole and I never declared corporate bankruptcy, some would say it was a failure.

If I had done things differently, I would not have had to experience the pain of that lesson. But because I did, I'm also a lot smarter now. No one at Rutgers taught me that if you grow your business, you can run out of cash. I was unprepared for the bite that growth was taking out of my cash flow. If I had hired a CFO, they could have told me I was burning through cash at an alarming rate, and I might want to raise some capital, before I try to grow so aggressively. Or, I could have sold the whole company, rather than the assets, before I ran out of cash. It was a valuable, expensive and painful lesson I don't wish on anyone. But like every other obstacle we face, they build character and arm us for the challenges to come.

Chapter Nine

Your Story Matters

– Adam Torres

"People don't care what you know, until they know that you care."

~Maya Angelou

I find it interesting that even some of the most accomplished and successful people tell me they don't think anybody cares about their story. These are people who have run million-dollar businesses, some even into hundreds of millions of dollars. I hear this when I interview them and when we are publishing them in our books.

People I meet, who have only ever thought about publishing a book, often say: "But who's going to read my book? Who really cares?" What I find fascinating is these are the same individuals who would watch or read other people's stories and they feel they are helped by those stories. Whether they are watching a YouTube video, a podcast or a documentary on Netflix, they feel informed and inspired by the content. But at the same time, they don't think other people will experience the same inspiration or help from their story. I find that incredibly interesting.

As humans, we all want and need the feeling of connection to others. We all crave the feeling that others have experienced what we've gone through, or are currently dealing with, especially when those people have made it to the other side.

A common story for an entrepreneur might be they bootstrapped their company or survived hard times. Maybe they lost everything or went bankrupt. I've heard stories of people having the lights turned off, and there they are, working by candlelight. Listening to stories about what people did to persevere, whether it was planning a new strategy, doing something that made them uncomfortable in terms of sales, or they had to get creative, inspires me to know they still figured it out. There is power and inspiration in the stories of people who have gone through the muck and made it to what they feel is success. These stories move us in ways dry facts and figures can't.

Why do these stories move us? Your voice and background will resonate differently with each person who hears it. Different parts of your story will resonate on different levels. Some will connect through geography. You're from New Jersey, they're from New Jersey. Others will connect based on growing up in a similar social or economic situation. Or it can be a million other things.

When I tell my own story about growing up in a middle-class family on the Southwest side of Detroit, some people key in on Motor City. I will tell people about starting out in the financial industry, leaving corporate America to start a media company. Some people key in on the financial industry. And now, I talk a lot about podcast production. Not everyone will connect with my story, but that's not the point. Some people will. They are my tribe. Others may need to hear a completely different story with a different voice and background to get the same message. They will find the tribe for them.

If you never tell your story and you keep it to yourself, I think that's a little selfish. The knowledge, experience and abilities you have are withheld, when they could be used to give something back, to teach someone something they need to hear. The person who needs to hear those lessons in a way only you can tell, will not be helped.

Monetary success is only one of the many story lines that move and inspire people. There are so many people who have survived stories of abuse, addiction or other tough challenges. By sharing their story, they open up possibilities for other people they could never have imagined.

The other side of success, which doesn't get talked about as much, is coping with it. I'm sure you've seen or heard of people who grew up in a great household, went to good schools and had plenty of money. On paper, everything looks just fine. But they have their own unique troubles in life. People assume they have it all figured out, but that person may feel like they shouldn't be telling their story. However, when they finally do tell their story, it empowers others who are just like them. A lot of people hear stunning stories of hardship and think they haven't gone through anything like that, but they are still having trouble. They still need help. Or, they might want to connect with someone like themselves.

One of my major or missions is to help individuals understand the importance of telling their story. Try not to think about the end result of telling your story. Just tell it. If you're writing a book, don't think about how or why you will tell it. Or about selling a million copies. Selling a million copies is not the point of writing a book, unless that's your revenue model and you've built up an audience and an entire company around it. The best reason to write a book is because you want to help people.

At the other end of writing a book, authors tell me the true gifts they received from the process of telling their story, and teaching from their authentic authority. They understand themselves on a deeper level. Their message gets crystalized in their mind and it becomes easier to communicate. Eventually, people say to me, "If this book helps one person, I'm happy I shared my story."

There is also a great deal of science, which is beyond my scope of knowledge, around why storytelling is powerful. The earliest form of human communication is storytelling that took place around prehistoric campfires. Stories were the primary vehicle for teaching, connecting and sharing news. Storytelling is a primordial act that is embedded in our human neurology. When you tell your story, you activate different parts of peoples' brains. Your story makes people feel more emotionally connected to you. We are programmed to learn through stories. And stories are how we move and inspire people.

Not everyone will be impressed or even like your story. However, that's not the point. The point is to attract your authentic tribe. The people who are your unique customers and fans will naturally be drawn to you from the telling of your story. Tim Ferris is a famous entrepreneur, investor, author, podcaster, and lifestyle guru. He is known for his four-hour self-help book series and is famous for saying your goal should be to attract 1,000 raving fans, not a million viewers. A smaller number of raving fans are far more powerful than a million lukewarm viewers. The raving fans will bring your message to everyone else for you. That has been the experience of Mission Matters. We've lived that. In fact, it's our business model.

Everyone's story is unique and often surprising. One of our authors, Darren Prince, shared his powerful story of outward success and inner turmoil. As a top Hollywood agent, with clients like Magic Johnson, Chevy Chase and Hulk Hogan, he was living what looked like a life of extreme success and notoriety. However, inwardly, he struggled with serious addiction issues. I wasn't expecting to hear that, and it reminded me that we are all human. Each of our stories humanize us. When we look at someone like Elon Musk, or anyone else in the news, we can make assumptions about them. But successful people have problems, too. Money isn't always the problem-solver we think it is.

There are so many more unique and amazing stories out there. I am continuously amazed by people's ingenuity and the incredible diversity of business ideas people create and use to support themselves and their families. I interviewed a man named John Charles Wilker on my podcast, who created what he calls The Simplest Biz. He makes millions flipping pallets and teaches others to do it, too. Companies who receive their goods on pallets often throw them away. Wilker collects them and resells them. Then, he designed a course to teach others how to start a simple business they could begin with very little money. He has helped many people become entrepreneurs, some making six figures, by flipping pallets.

He has a thriving Facebook community of people helping and inspiring each other. It's amazing.

I made the mistake of not telling my story when I started out in the financial advisory side of things. I thought I could get up there and talk about the business I was in, and how we help people, then they would line up and buy the products. That's not the way it works. Of course, in the investment advisory world of corporate presentations, nobody wants to hear about my childhood. But they do need to hear a little about what I've done in the financial realm, in order to establish my credibility. You can and should tailor your story to fit your audience, industry and the time constraints. I wasn't doing any of that back then, I was only sharing the facts.

After I published my first book, people started inviting me to speak. I didn't understand what I was doing wrong, so I started working with a mentor, who told me I have to share my story. I was similar to many of my own clients now, who ask why would I want to share my story. I didn't understand it. After he explained the why to me, I began to notice how successful speakers share a bit of their story before jumping into the content. I felt inspired by other people's stories and it made me wonder, if I was being inspired by other people's stories, couldn't others be inspired by mine?

Once I started sharing my own story and who I was as a person, it shocked me when people cared. They wanted to know about me and it brought them closer to me. I had no idea the idea of sharing in a business atmosphere would connect people in an emotional way. I didn't understand how it worked, until I did it. When you share your story, people warm up to you. They feel connected to you. And, you feel more connected to your audience. It's reciprocal. Sharing my story from the stage, I can see people change as I'm talking. Their eyes and even their body language softens a little. They become more relaxed in their chairs.

Then it becomes interesting when you meet someone for the first time, and they already know your story. You start to ask yourself, how do they know that? Then you realize, you talked about it on a podcast!

In the podcast format, such as ours and many others, assuming you're not an A-List celebrity who is already known to the masses, we always begin with the invited person telling a little bit about their background, so our audience knows who they are and has time to connect and warm up to them. It's not by accident. It's by design. People want to know why they should listen to someone, and their story and background answers these questions in their mind, so they can settle in and really listen.

Once you've decided to tell your story in whatever way you feel comfortable and whatever setting you deem appropriate, it's important to tell it correctly. The most important advice to remember is to understand the timing and format you have to work with. For example, if you're going to be on TV and you have a three-minute spot, you can still tell your story, you just have to be quick. It might only be a sentence. If an interviewer asked me, "Adam, what are your thoughts on the future trends in your book publishing business?" Knowing I don't have much time, I can fit a bit of my story in like this:

> "I grew up reading books in Detroit, Michigan, and I loved reading about Henry Ford, his background and how he grew the automobile industry. Just like the automobile industry was thriving for a long time, then had a bit of trouble and had to redefine itself, I think publishing is doing the same thing. We have to constantly redefine our business and monetary models, as more and more bookstores close. Are we going to sell on websites? Or are we going to sell more on Kindle? But like the auto industry, people are still driving cars and they are still reading books."

In that short answer, I was able to share a bit of my background and personality within the context of answering the question, without derailing anything. That's TV. There's no warm up, but you still have to accomplish your goal.

If you're doing a keynote speech and you have 20 or 30 minutes, you have more time to present your story and connect with your audience emotionally. You will want to craft your story, then create different versions for the different platforms where you deliver your content.

Let's discuss the most popular platforms where you may find yourself telling your story and trying to connect with the audience. The platforms will range from about 15 seconds on TikTok, up to about four hours on a long webinar or half day bootcamp. Within every one of these formats, you will have different opportunities to craft your story in ways that will connect with the different audiences.

On TikTok, you might have three or four seconds to work in a few sentences sharing a little about who you are. Then, the rest is content. When you're doing three to five minutes on TV, that's a different game, and gives you a little more time like the example I shared above. For a 20-minute keynote, you may want to get your story down to a few minutes, which is longer than you think. Another unique opportunity is speaking on a panel. How do you answer a question, while also adding in a little about your story and still making it feel natural, without derailing the discussion?

When you're on a podcast, you will usually start with your background. If you're on a live stream, you could share your story by asking questions, then relating to your audience's answers in a way that engages them. I was taught how to do this by qualified people who specialize in the different platforms I've mentioned. If you plan on doing a lot of public speaking, you might consider investing in similar training.

Aside from fear, one of the things that keep people from telling their story is getting caught up in what format they should be developing. There are so many ways to distribute your story. Should you do a podcast, write a book or do a Facebook Live? Analysis paralysis is a real thing, and it keeps many people from telling their story for years.

I'm here to tell you it doesn't matter what platform you use. Allow yourself to be flexible and if it doesn't work, try something else. Try different platforms, until you find one you like. Even though everyone seems to be on TikTok it doesn't mean that's where you should be. You should always do what feels comfortable to you. If you don't want to do video, you can start a blog. Somewhere in the world, someone started a blog today that will end up being huge for the audience it is targeting. It is not because blogs are new and novel. They're not. The reason that specific blog will be successful is because that person is telling their story,creating authentic content around a unique topic and within a unique niche.

I have experimented on a lot of different platforms. Some of them don't even exist anymore. As you go through the learning process of telling your own story on various platforms, you will discover what feels comfortable and authentic to you. Do what feels good and right for you. If you try something that looks good for someone else, but it doesn't feel good to you, don't be afraid to stop and try something else. Maybe an entire book is too much for you. If that's the case, try writing a short ebook. If you don't like to write and you want to talk, try a podcast. Maybe you would instead enjoy telling your story through pictures on Instagram. Telling your story through pictures is reminiscent of the old Life magazines.

You don't have to be on every platform, and you don't have to do everything at the same time. The main thing is to just start. You will be shocked and surprised by the responses you get. People will begin telling you, "That really helped me," or "That inspired me," or "I needed to hear that today." These responses will affirm the power of telling your story and help you in the storytelling journey.

Once you've put yourself out there and told your story, this is when the real work begins. You have to continue to tell your story. Don't be like most people who write a book and then never talk about it. Don't create a podcast, do a couple of episodes, then stop. When you continue to tell your story, that's when you will see the amazing long-term effects.

Telling your story eventually becomes a fluid thing, and will become easier the more you share. It also can be accomplished in any format and in any medium.

The problem is continuing to tell their story and share, because this becomes the challenge for most people telling their story. However, the mistake most people make is not telling it at all. I was in that exact boat when I started out. It wasn't until I went through my own transformation and saw what happened when I did share my story that I understood the magnitude of sharing it. That's what made me fall in love with this whole idea of telling your story. And, that's why I now help other people tell their stories. The point is, just tell your story.

Chapter Ten

Deal with What Is

– Elliot Kallen

"People often say that motivation doesn't last. Well, neither does bathing—that's why we recommend it daily."

~Zig Ziglar

Like so many entrepreneurs, I live on the edge of stress. I can get hyper and frazzled. I have one hour to be with you and in 59 minutes, I'm going to turn into a pumpkin. And in 61 minutes, I'm going to have 11 people in my office! The best thing to mitigate stress is fun.

When I had my company back east, I used to shut the whole thing down for a long weekend and take everyone to the Epcot Center at Walt Disney World in Florida. It's different from Disneyland in California. Epcot has world's fair style pavilions. One showcases the Land, one showcases the Seas, and others showcase different countries. The one called the Land was amazing. It showed the history of Earth. As we were going through, we started to smell something, which was a swamp smell. Then, the dinosaurs appeared. And eventually, they became oil. That exhibit excited all of our senses: sight, smell, sound and visuals. It was so creative. If we all could be half as creative as Disney, imagine how successful we could be.

Once I moved to California, we created a culture of fun there, too. Everyone in my office eats together two or three days a week. And we make fun of each other. I am 220 pounds, I have a 49-inch chest and big broad shoulders. You can dump just about anything on me and I'll survive. Most of the time, they're laughing at me and that's okay, because I have big shoulders. I love when they love to make fun of me and when we make fun of each other. Our office setting is a culture of fun. And, we also really talk to each other. We get into the personal stuff, and support and care for each other.

When somebody makes a mistake, which is daily, because that's what happens in business, we have trained ourselves and each other to own the mistake. That's a big thing in my mind. If you make a mistake, own it and then let's work at fixing it. And after it's all over, we explore what we learned from that mistake. Then, we can laugh about it.

The thought process is, "I screwed up today. My job is still okay. I can still do it. I have to get a little better at my job. I know I can do this and my team is supportive of me. Let's be better tomorrow." We talk about how we can improve on a regular basis. And when we have meetings, we talk about what went wrong last week, and how we can fix that process. Being able to talk about our mistakes creates a feeling of safety and growth, where people want to stay with you. I like working with people who actually want to be here. As a consequence, we don't have a high turnover rate.

Sometimes, you learn lessons from your parents, because they share them with you and sometimes, you learn by observing them. One of the major things I observed about my dad was his incredible work ethic. He was born in 1915 and lived through the depression, sleeping on a cold floor in a flat, having nothing and pooling money from other families to get enough food to eat. That was pretty standard growing up in Newark, N.J., at that time. The Greatest Generation had to have a great work ethic. Today's 21-year-old workers entering the business world don't have anywhere near the same work ethic.

Without my dad meaning to, he passed it on to his three kids. We all work five and a half to six and a half days a week on average, because we like working. Dad had a powerful family-oriented work ethic. He worked hard all week, and Sunday was family day. The downside of his work ethic was that he failed to create any good hobbies. His mother taught him that life is work and work is life, and hobbies and sports are for children. I think that's terrible advice, but he lived by that credo. On his day off, instead of doing something for himself, he would do something for his family. It was a wonderful thing to do, especially for his two boys, who were really into sports.

When professional baseball player Mickey Mantle was close to retirement, my brother and I were gigantic Yankees fans. I never saw Mickey Mantle at his best, because I was too young. But I remember when they had Mickey Mantle Day at the old Yankees Stadium. It had pillars where, if you sat behind one, you had to move your head to see. The game was sold out, but my dad got us tickets. We were pretty high up, but it didn't matter. He got what he could afford to take his two sons to the game and we were thrilled.

There were 60,000 people in the stands, and during the seventh- inning stretch, they gave Mickey Mantle a Cadillac. Then, at the bottom of the eighth inning, the Yankees were down by two runs, with two men on base. Mickey Mantle came up to the plate and we knew he was going to hit a home run and win the game. He didn't, but we were screaming and punching each other in the arms anyway.

Normally, we weren't allowed to do that. When we realized our dad wasn't stopping us from pounding each other, we turned to look at him. Close to 60,000 people were on their feet screaming, "Mick! Mick! Mick!" And there was Dad, fast asleep, snoring away. I remember my brother and I looking at each other and feeling sorry for our dad, who had to work all the time so he could take us to a Yankees game. It was a revelation at a young age—there's more to life than work, even though you need to work and take care of your family. We also understood he would do anything to take care of his family.

Taking care of your family is important and it requires discipline. The best tool you can have as an entrepreneur is discipline. I get up at 4:45 every morning and hit the gym. However, I haven't always done that. In March 2021, we canceled our planned trip to Europe, due to the COVID-19 pandemic, and decided to go to Alaska instead. Shortly before our trip, I met with my doctor. He said, "You've got borderline high blood pressure, your back is killing you and you're sitting here sweating, because you can't touch your toes. You need to either lose 30 pounds, or I'm putting you on permanent medicine." I told him when I got back from Alaska, I'd start the doctor-supervised diet.

The trip I planned to Alaska was very outdoorsy and physical. My wife asked me if I could do it and I told her that I didn't know. Admitting I couldn't do something was a very hard thing for me to do. In Denali, we took a helicopter up to 11,000 feet. We were in heavy boots and gear, because it was about 45 degrees. Walking on this tundra was like walking on a thick sponge. Your feet would sink about four to six inches with every step. It was a lot of work.

I was coming up last, so I told everyone, including my wife, to go on ahead. I told them that I would catch up to them. I was totally out of breath at that altitude, drenched in sweat and lagging way behind the group. I was struggling so much, I thought to myself, if I had a heart attack and died hiking Denali National Park, it wouldn't be the worst thing. Then, my wife came back for me, and said, "You're not doing well here. Do you want to get a helicopter out?" I said, no. I felt terrible, but I was going to do this. We slowly walked the rest of the way. At that moment, I told myself, I would never be this out of shape again.

I have always been a big guy. But due to COVID-19 shutdowns, and not going to the gym, because it was closed, and eating potato chips and other garbage foods, I had gained 30 pounds. The day after we got home from Alaska, I went to the doctor's office and started a keto diet. Over the next two months, I lost 30 pounds and I'm now working on the next 15.

I've had four back surgeries, which means I can't lift weights off the ground, but I can do machines and I can walk on a treadmill. Now, my goal in the gym is to burn 1,000 calories by seven every morning of the week. My original goal was to have one chin. When people used to ask me how much weight I wanted to lose, I'd say one chin. Diet and exercise has helped me create more discipline in my life. To be a great entrepreneur, you need to have discipline.

Some engineers have unbelievable discipline, beyond what you and I will ever have, because they are so methodical. They do nothing without discipline. But entrepreneurs are not always like that. We are free-thinkers. We're creative, in the flow, big picture people. When that type of person doesn't have discipline, they can jump from big picture to big picture. Without details, they become all talk and no action. It is important to get the little things done today, in order to have the big picture tomorrow.

If you're having trouble with any of these lifestyle issues, try hiring a coach. I did a lot of Anthony Robbins live events when I was younger. He talked a lot about discipline, but it can be hard to do on your own. Hiring a coach helps, because you can't give them the same excuses you give yourself. They also provide a counter narrative to the naysayers, who inevitably show up whenever you set a big goal or seek to elevate what you're doing.

Negative family members and friends are an unfortunate probability in life. Some of the most well-meaning people in the world want the best for themselves, and they disguise it as the best for you. I have a sister who is the most negative person I've ever met in my life. She could walk into a room and say something like, "Any one of these ceiling tiles could fall down on you and you'd have a lawsuit." She could find the most negative possibility anywhere. She was an assistant district attorney in New Jersey. It was a perfect job for her, because their world is so negative.

According to people like this, when you're in business, it can only end in failure. When you're in a marriage, it can only end in divorce. To this day, she still blames me for my son's suicide, because I sent him to a cold state to go to college, instead of a warm state. She blames a lot of her life's problems on our parents, because according to her, they didn't do a good enough job raising her.

I remember when my parents were trying to kick my sister out of the house. She had moved home after college and was in her 40s at the time. Mom and dad were buying everything, including all her food. We were all having dinner together one night, when my brother and I suggested she get her own place. My parents thought it sounded like a healthy idea. She started yelling at them: "You kick me out of this house, and I'll commit suicide! It'll be on your shoulders for life!"

Of course, my parents backed down immediately. She was so personally strong as a lawyer and she scared a lot of people. That was her job and she was good at it. She was well versed as a prosecutor in reading people and what they meant to say, versus what they actually said when they were lying. She knew how to trap people in a lie, and how to make them feel bad about what they were doing. If you went to her and told her you wanted to start a business, she was going to find the negative zipper to the black lining of that pillow.

I learned when my family asked about my business, I talked very little about it, because I knew where the conversation would go. When I first started out in the financial services business, it was hard getting started in a new place, where I had no contacts.

If I had gone to her, and said, "I'm really struggling," she would say, "You need to get a job."

My brother used to say, "You've got to give up this dream and get a job."

Even my ex-wife said, "Maybe your dream is all wrong. You should get a job. We need money."

They were all well-meaning, but I stuck with it anyway, against all their well-meaning conversations, and I'm glad I did.

Conversely, I also had family members who were in my corner and rooting for me. They were always asking what they could do to help. Several of my family members were my biggest supporters and I am thankful for them.

I never lost sight of my vision and my dream, even though I had naysayers. I had a big picture idea and it was malleable. I knew I wanted to create something one day that would be a saleable entity I could walk away from. I wanted to say I built it from scratch, took it the whole lifecycle and then sold it.

I'm still in that growth cycle. Not a day goes by that I don't want to continue growing, getting bigger and achieving better. I've never been good with the status quo. I will never go home satisfied with today. I might be thrilled with something that happened today, but I will never be someone who is satisfied with not growing. Even if something great happens today, I'll still go home wanting to be better tomorrow.

You should relish and revel in your successes. It keeps you hungry for more. If you're just starting out as an entrepreneur, it helps to understand that not every business starts with a boom. Most start small. Even huge companies like Facebook and Amazon were nothing like they are today, when they started.

Bill Gates originally tried to sell the DOS operating system to IBM, but they wouldn't buy it. They didn't see any value in a home computer, because they were business to business. So, he went back to Seattle and created Microsoft. He decided, if no one was going to buy their product, they would just do it themselves. Apple already had a lot of market penetration in what would become the personal computer market. However, both companies had a really slow start. The trick is to not lose your vision, no matter how slow your start is.

When I moved to California, and started at Lincoln Financial, I had to get a job at 24 Hour Fitness at night, because I needed money. When my supportive family members asked me, what could they do to help me succeed, I asked them if they knew anyone in California. And if they knew anyone who knew anyone in California. Eventually, I talked to people, but it was a painful stretch.

Starting a business doesn't always start with success. It sometimes starts with your nose getting bloodied every day. You have to focus on the yeses and the positives, and not focus on the nos and the bloody noses. Slow starts are indicative of successful companies. Sometimes, fast starts can be the big shining star that's here today and gone tomorrow. Slow starts are built, brick by brick, until they finally get momentum.

During that initial push, while you're trying not to lose your vision, also make sure you don't lose yourself. Don't lose your character. You need to exude and exhibit good character, because that's what makes people trust you. Trust is the hardest thing to acquire, and the fastest thing to lose. In the money business, it's all about trust. Every business eventually comes down to trust. Have you ever wanted to buy a product that was advertised on social media by someone you don't know, and you check to see if it's sold on Amazon instead, because you don't want to trust your credit card to a stranger? That's trust.

You must always avoid bribes and kickbacks. If you sell your soul once, it's very hard to get that trust back. If I made you 40-percent on the stock market in one year, but you didn't trust me, you would still leave me. If someone says, "He's doing a great job. That's why I'm with him." That's not true. You're with him, because you trust him. And, he happens to be doing a great job. Those are two different things.

Sometimes, things happen that are simply beyond your control. That's the nature of business and something you have to deal with as a business owner or entrepreneur. When I was an advisor at Raymond James, a client came to me with a lot of stock. She was an early headhunter in Silicon Valley, who had been paid heavily in stock. She had a lot of shares of Sun Microsystems and Nortel, and wanted to park her stock with me. Her stock grew very quickly to a valuation of about $6 million. I wasn't even charging her. This was a freebie. My partner and I tried to convince her that she needed to diversify and she yelled at us: "You don't understand the new economy! The old economy is dead!" Of course, in 2000, the market tanked and those two companies don't even exist anymore.

Over the years, she had been leveraging that stock to pay taxes and purchase real estate, by borrowing on margin. With margin, you eventually have to pay the piper, and she started getting margin calls on her $6 million. It only took about five months until she finally sold everything and her $6 million was down to about $600,000.

In the meantime, we had been sending out emails to clients every week to keep them informed. This was the early days of email, and Raymond James put us on heightened alert for sending out too many emails to clients. They thought too many emails meant something was wrong. We changed our system and went down to one a week, which I did on Sunday nights.

This woman and her husband filed a lawsuit against us for the $6 million in stock losses, plus punitive damages of another $6 million. Their excuse was they were never told the margin would have to be repaid. She and her husband ran a company, and both had MBAs. And they signed margin agreements, but they claimed they signed whatever we put in front of them.

Raymond James decided their lawyers would represent us, and it was the only way they would have it. At the end of the day, the mediator found there was no basis for the lawsuit.

Unfortunately, the mediator decided we should pay all of Raymond James' legal fees, plus the cost of the Raymond James lawyers coming from Florida to California, as well as the couple's legal fees. We won, but it cost us $150,000; $100,000 was paid by insurance and my business partner and I had to come up with $50,000. We didn't want to settle, but Raymond James said if we didn't take the deal, they were going to fire us on Monday morning, and we would be out of the industry for cause.

We felt like we did nothing wrong, but we were forced to take the deal. We never made a dime on any of that stock. We didn't buy it, and we didn't sell it. We only parked it. She signed agreements, and we met with her to recommend she sell it. Meanwhile, this little unfortunate incident is permanently on our records.

A month later, my partner was in San Francisco, meeting with the sales manager for Raymond James. He said they were thinking about kicking us out of the company, because we "lost" that lawsuit. He shot back, "We didn't even want to settle. We did nothing wrong." The sales manager replied, "Yeah, but you cost us $100,000 from our insurance pool."

After I heard about that conversation, I flew to Florida to meet with the sales manager and we had a nice conversation. He agreed to not kick us out, but we knew our days were numbered. Luckily, Schwab walked into our office shortly after and we moved away from Raymond James completely.

You could view the whole debacle as a gigantic negative. We were almost kicked out of the industry for something that was not our fault. But those are the kinds of things you face sometimes when you're in business. You have to deal with what is, and when you do it enough times, you eventually become a business leader.

CHAPTER ELEVEN

LEADERSHIP IS NOT GLAMOROUS

– ELLIOT KALLEN

"If your actions inspire others to dream more, learn more, do more, and become more, you are a leader."

~Simon Sinek

Leadership is not usually intuitive. It's a skill that has to be practiced and learned. And the younger you learn, the better. Leadership is one more thing we don't encourage enough in young people. There is a leadership group at every high school, but it's almost always made up of 10 or 20 of the coolest kids. I was not on the leadership council at school, because I found another outlet.

At the beginning of tenth grade, I was pulling away from my boyhood friends and making new friends. Of course, my hormones were raging and I had no idea what to do with all that energy. I was home on a Saturday, pacing around the house, when my dad asked me what was going on. I said, "I'm not friends with those guys anymore. I don't want to go over to their house and play pool and order pizza anymore. I just feel like I need more." He asked me who my best friend was at that moment. That was Richie. I explained to my dad, Richie joined a youth leadership group called AZA, and they would go to parties all around northern New Jersey on weekends. My dad told me to call Richie and tell him I wanted to go to next week's party, so I did. Richie said, "Great. We'll pick you up."

I immediately got involved with the group and shortly thereafter, there were elections for the new board. Richie wanted to run for president, and he suggested I take over as programming vice president. We ran together and that was the beginning of leadership for me.

That summer, AZA hosted a leadership camp. I told my dad I wanted to go, but he didn't have the money, and he was busy with my mom, who was very sick. But he told me there was an organization called Rotary that sometimes would give out money to kids for leadership training. He told me to knock on the door of a man named Lester Block. I was scared to death, but I did it.

He was an older man who was nice, but intimidating. He invited me in and told me to sit down. He said, "Tell me what you're trying to accomplish." I told him about myself and what I wanted to do. He told me he would think about it and that my knocking on his door said a lot about me. This was a big lesson at a young age. It is important to step outside of your comfort zone. The next day, he called my parents and told me I could pick up a check the next day.

The leadership camp gave me an entire summer of leadership classes. They taught me how to set goals, how to motivate other people to help me reach my goals, and how to listen to others and help them reach their goals. We also learned to think innovatively. Just because it's never been done before, doesn't mean it can't be done. I learned to think about the end goal first. Ask yourself when setting these goals, how you want that to look for you and your business. Then, think about how it can be accomplished. If you monitor your business goals and make adjustments as needed, you can create things.

I went to a high school that didn't have any sports leagues. Our group put together a football league, and later, a baseball league. There were no social programs organized either, so we put those together, too. Our little 12-person AZA organization in West Orange, N.J., suddenly became 60, because we created a reputation that we were fun, we played sports and we didn't judge.

Then, we decided we had to give back. We started doing car washes and all the money we made went to charity. We visited nursing homes and spent time with people. Most of them wanted to hold your hand and talk. They wanted to hear all the stories about our lives. If it was a Jewish home, I brought a shofar, which is a ram's horn you blow on Rosh Hashanah. Many of them couldn't go to synagogue anymore, so I would blow the horn for them.

In college, I was asked by the Dean of Student Affairs at Rutgers University to be the constitutional expert for the student council. I had to memorize the Constitution of the Student Leadership of Rutgers, and become familiar with the U.S. Constitution. The Dean got me to do it, because he understood my situation. I was struggling with trying to work 40 hours a week and keep up with school, while most of my friends were having a much better time. I stayed active in the leadership team and didn't really think twice about it at the time. Sometimes, leadership means doing the things you have to do, not only the things you want to do.

While I often sought out leadership opportunities, being invited to fill leadership roles like the one at Rutgers has been crucial to developing leadership skills. As a leader, I want to invite others into roles that will develop their skills, too. I've always been a big fan of trying to initiate creativity from my team. One of the biggest problems with small business owners is they want to make themselves the most important person there. As a result, they hire people who are less smart, less aggressive or less threatening than they are.

This was a real problem for my dad. He used to tell me, "If you hire someone as good as you, he will eventually steal your business." When I was looking for a job after I closed my packaging supplies business, I went on a lot of interviews. Two companies specifically interviewed me multiple times. And both of them gave me the same reason for not hiring me. They both said, "At some point, you will steal our clients and go into your own business." Both of them found being bright and aggressive a threat.

The lesson in that was, if you're confident in yourself, you want to hire better talent than you. Surround yourself with great talent. The danger with that is, yes, they can leave you and start their own company. It's done every day in this country, and especially in my industry. But if you create a culture worth staying at, with participation and equity, then you strengthen your company. I've always been that person. I always try to hire someone who is better or smarter than me at something. Do you hire to your strengths or do you hire to your weaknesses?

When I was younger, I thought I should hire to my strengths, so we become even stronger. But actually, you want to hire people who can do things you can't do. Especially in sales. If you hire someone who is better than you, they will light it up.

My dad had an interesting opportunity in the 1960s. He had just started to sell industrial spray paint in his little business. Spray paint was not in retail yet. It was primarily used in the steel industry to color code steel bars and other similar materials. One of the major players in the industry came to my father, and said, "You're one of the few people who understands the spray paint industry." They offered him an exclusive spray paint contract for the state of New Jersey.

That would have grown his company tenfold. He would have had to hire a bunch of people and do other things outside of his comfort zone. I remember my mom and dad had quite an argument about doing this. Do we grow or not? Could this grow, or is it a waste of money? Could it bankrupt us? They decided not to do it, because they thought spray paint would never take off in this country. No one would get rid of the brush.

Obviously, that was a bad decision. He made that decision out of fear. He didn't want to do something he didn't understand. He wasn't willing to lead. He had no vision to imagine, what if it actually works? A lot of entrepreneurs make decisions out of fear. Or they make decisions not to succeed, because what would people think of them? What would their family think? What about the naysayers? We all have this habit of buying into criticism from people we care about. If someone tells you your glasses are the wrong color for you, you suddenly look in the mirror and wonder if you bought the wrong glasses.

There was an experiment done at a high school that revealed the power of your friends. The premise of the experiment was all set up. The first person would come up to someone and ask, "Hey, are you feeling okay today?" And they would say, "I'm feeling great." Half an hour later, someone else would come up to that same person and ask, "Hey, how do you feel today?" And they would say, "I'm okay." By the time the third person did this to that same person, they would begin to wonder if they don't look good anymore. And by the fourth time, that person would be going home sick.

People can create doubt in your mind, both knowingly and unknowingly, and that can create a culture of failure. One of the most important things a leader can do is to create a culture of success. Personally, I want more than success. I want to create a culture of fun, success and creativity.

One of the most powerful ways a leader can create a culture of success is to mentor people. But it's equally important to get a mentor, even as a leader.

When I started my first business, I did not understand the need to find a mentor. I was super young, 24 years old and I think it was a rookie mistake. No matter what you're doing, find someone who is successful and has a personality compatible with yours, in order to learn how they do things. By not having a mentor, I ended up completely reinventing the wheel and doing things the hard way. The hard way means it takes extra energy, extra labor and extra money to get to the same place.

A mentor is someone who has been doing the job you want to do for 10 or 20 years and can share their experiences with you. If you're a teacher, find a teacher who is really good and emulate what they do. When I started in the financial services business, I already understood the need for a mentor. I began talking to people who were in this business, and who dealt with business owners, which was my focus. They started to give me feedback.

Some of it was incredibly helpful, and some of it was negative. They told me not to do something, but I thought they were wrong. Sometimes, I did it anyway and it worked for me, because I understood my personality was different from theirs. I always like to do things my own way, and even though I had a mentor, I weighed their feedback against my personality to create something that would work for me. I would be a terrible McDonald's franchise owner, because I can make a better hamburger than they can. I can't sell 35 billion of them, but I can make a better hamburger.

I think everybody needs to find a mentor in business who can be a buddy. Find a buddy who is good at what you do. Maybe you're better at some things and they are better at others. If you want to be a better golfer, find a mentor who is better at golf than you to practice and play with, so you can learn from them. You want to find someone who can teach you some of the ropes and shortcuts. Find out what mistakes they made, so you don't have to make the same ones.

One of the best examples of this is Alcoholics Anonymous (AA). What is the first thing they do when you join AA? They set you up with someone who has already gone through it. If you can't find a mentor, you can always hire a mentor. Hire a consultant. I always hire someone to help me with my public speaking. I have joined with some mentors from Los Angeles and Las Vegas to help my foundation become a national charity. We meet every Monday to talk about how to get on TV, radio and podcasts. They are great mentors, because they have their own production companies and they've done what I'm trying to accomplish.

Mentorship is all about finding an expert, paid or otherwise, who does what you want to do better than you do, and who feels similar to you. You don't necessarily want to be a copycat, but in some cases, that does work. Once you find someone you can learn from, you can filter that information through your own personality.

You can go on the internet and find more research than you could ever consume about how to be a success. But that vast information is only two dimensional. I would rather talk to five people who have actually done exactly what I want to do.

When I was doing environmental cleanup work, I needed to find a mentor, because I knew so little about it. A man named John Spencer had been doing that kind of work for a long time. He was a lot like the former President Lyndon Baines Johnson (LBJ), who was six-foot-four with piercing blue eyes. He was so tall, he looked down on most people and could be incredibly intimidating. Similar to LBJ, John Spencer was six-foot-five, blue eyes, big gray ostrich cowboy boots, and he had a look about him that was pure intimidation.

I'm certainly not intimidating by any means. I'm built like a small vending machine. You'll have a hard time knocking me over.

I asked John one time, how he was such a good closer of business all the time. He said, "It's all in the eyes. You have to make strong eye contact and not look away. I have piercing eyes. I stare right at them and they know I'm not lying. I don't have to say I'm not lying. They know it."

When I was looking for mentors, I wondered what I could learn from John Spencer. Not all of his values were redeeming, but when he was out there, he was always telling the truth. People knew he was sincere. When he was in your face, he was doing it for the right reason. If you're sincere about wanting to learn, you can learn something from everyone. The message here is to go find a mentor. Even if they're different from you, you will learn something from them.

One of the important jobs of a mentor is to motivate people. As a leader or business owner, your job is to motivate people to do a better job. Some people need to be motivated daily. There are two types of motivation: positive motivation and negative motivation. When you talk to your team, you will find out which one they get turned on by.

Let me give you an example of the difference between the two.

"If you can get this big task done by the end of the month, I have a $100 bill waiting for you." Or it could be a trip or a $1,000 shopping spree. That's positive motivation.

"If you keep eating those doughnuts, you're going to be a fat blob." That's negative motivation. That may sound harsh, but for some people, it works.

When I was at Lincoln, they tried to figure me out. I'm a positive motivation guy. If you dangle a trip or some award, I'm going to like it and work for it. I like recognition and I like to win trips. I like taking my wife on trips, and I always enjoyed telling my kids we were going on a trip when they were at home. But every now and then, they would walk in, point the finger at me and berate me. "If you don't do this, you're going to look like a loser." I know it works for some people, but I truly believe most people are positively motivated.

The same principles apply at your office. If you want your office staff members to be better, you have to think about how to positively motivate them. There's an interesting movie called, *Glengarry Glen Ross*, which is all about sales. In one particular scene, the character played by Alec Baldwin berated one of his salesmen. It's the essence of de-motivation. As entrepreneurs, we have to be careful not to demotivate people. I would start with positive motivation. You can ask people if they like to travel. Where do they like to go? Then when you find out what they like most you can say, "If you accomplish this big thing, I'll help you get that trip."

I did this recently with my assistant. She said she wanted to go to Mexico, but she couldn't afford it. I told her if we get this one case, which was so complex and had a lot of moving parts, I'd send her to Mexico. She worked her tail off helping me to get that case. I bought her a trip and off she went to Puerto Vallarta.

As leaders, we also have to motivate ourselves. Fear of failure can be as much of a motivator as the drive for success. When I started my packaging company, I was so young. When you're that young, you don't really know anything. You're merely working on pure instinct. I was calling people every night and my brother, who was my roommates, was in awe of how I kept calling people and kept getting rejected. I had a drive for success. I knew it was a numbers game. If I wanted to get two sales, I had to call 20 people. You have to get the numbers to work on your side. You have to make it happen. Later in my career, the numbers game became second nature to me.

The financial services business typically has a low threshold of success. Over 95-percent of startups burn out in five years. It's staggering, almost to the point of being dumb. I was making a hundred calls a day in the beginning. I'm not sure if it was a drive for success or a fear of failure. I decided, with a set of twins and a little baby at home, I could not fail.

When you look at entrepreneurial motivations, you have to ask yourself which is the greater drive for you: the drive for success or the fear of failure. Most people think we are wired for one or the other. I think we are wired for both, depending on how you look at it. You may think, I'm going to do this to succeed, but I know if I don't do that, I will fail. It works both ways. It's kind of like going to the gym to lose 20 pounds. If I eat potato chips all day, I'm not fearing failure. But if I'm getting married in three months and I get an ultimatum saying I need to lose 20 pounds to fit in my tuxedo or she's not marrying me, you can bet I'm going to be at the gym and the potato chips will not be in my cabinet.

Some people think a fear of failure is a greater motivation than the drive for success, because we'll do anything not to fail. You won't always do what it takes to succeed, but you will do things to avoid failure. However, it's mission critical for an entrepreneur to be motivated by both. Do what you need to do to succeed, and make sure you don't do those things that make you fail. It's all about finding balance.

Chapter Twelve

Balance is an Illusion

– Elliot Kallen

"Next to love, balance is the most important thing."

~John Wooden

There are four areas of life we need to keep in balance: work, spouse, parenthood and our physical health. As an entrepreneur, you can't help but want to work 50 to 60 hours a week. Some work less and some more, but the point is, you're building your baby. Your company is like your child. If you're married and have children, something is going to give. You're either going to be a lesser spouse or a lesser parent.

On any given day, your life will be out of balance on one of these four things. You need to think through what needs to be in balance right at that moment and make it a priority. For example, today, I'm going to be an entrepreneur all day, but tomorrow is Friday and I'm going home early so I can play dad. Or another example, I can take everybody out to dinner, or I can be a good spouse.

Wherever I am, I need to be present. When we're so busy trying to build something, it's easy to not be present. When you're under high stress, you don't always eat the best food or take time for exercise. Entrepreneurs tend to be high coffee drinkers or soda drinkers, and they eat at their desks, shoving down sandwiches and potato chips.

It can be unpleasant and lonely to be a leader, because you're making tough decisions. You cannot be a great leader, a great father and a great husband all at the same time. You're spinning plates in the air, while trying to keep them all spinning. But you're not excelling at all of them. There will always be a first, a second and a third place.

What happens if your company is number one and being a great dad is number three? Who's going to suffer? Your kids. What if being a great husband is number three? Your marriage will suffer. What if you make your company number three and go be a great dad and husband, which are two very worthy causes, because you can't ever get that time back. But what if your company fails, because you're not giving it the attention, effort and energy it deserves?

You cannot do all four main areas well at the same time. You have to make difficult choices on a day-to-day basis. And you have to remember those choices. Maybe today, you need to get out of the office and be a great dad. Tomorrow, you can be a great business owner and entrepreneur. Or, you get to do the dad part at six o'clock. You have to balance the areas out consciously. If it's unconscious, the loudest voice will get your attention, and then you'll be putting out fires every day. That's why there's a high divorce rate among entrepreneurs.

You will always be out of balance, every day. But remember, it's only one day. You create balance over time.

One of the best tools to help you succeed at life's balancing act is humor. It's important to maintain a sense of humor. In business and in life, you will face adversaries and adversarial situations on a regular basis. The first thing you should do every day as an entrepreneur is look in the mirror and laugh. You're human. You're going to make mistakes every day. I make mistakes every day. And I am always apologizing to somebody on my team.

I think laughing at yourself is a good thing. Encourage your team to laugh with you, and sometimes maybe even at you. We're all quirky in our own way, and it's the quirkiness that makes life so interesting. Relish it and it will help you to thrive. Your quirkiness can be your greatest strength. What's enjoyable about people is our differences. Some are slightly different, and others are 180 degrees different. Make those differences joyful, because they're your alter ego.

Laugh at yourself. Laugh with others and allow them to laugh at you. And when you're alone, put on a comedy or listen to comedians. If you're fighting a serious illness, one of the best things you can do is watch comedy shows. When I eat lunch at my desk, I still watch Abbott and Costello routines. It changes my whole mental state. It's amazing what "Who's on First" can do for your mentality. When my kids were young, I made them memorize the whole "Who's on First" routine. It's 25 minutes long. To this day, I can say to my kids, "What's the name of the guy on second base?" They respond, "Who." It's automatic. It reminds us to lighten up, it is really serious. As a species, we are over the top stressed out. No other species is as stressed out as we are. It's important to maintain a sense of humor.

My wife is a blonde and she is the first person to tell you when she has a blonde moment. I make fun of myself all the time. I say, "Look, I'm short, white and Jewish. What do you want from me?" That's much more fun than saying, "My whole life, I was picked on, because I was the shortest kid in the class." With the second statement, you're claiming victimhood. There's a difference between humor and victimhood. No one likes to be around a victim. Make it okay to poke a little bit of fun at yourself sometimes to combat the stresses of life.

Humor and fun are tools for creating balance in your life. But fun doesn't just happen. You have to plan for it like you would plan anything else. If you want to have a good life, it takes planning. If you want to have a great retirement, it takes planning. When I became an adult, I always worked my butt off.

About a decade ago, I sat down with my wife, Tammy, and told her every day, I advise my clients about how to have a successful retirement. Almost every time, they come from the perspective of money. They want to know, will they have enough money for their retirement. That was the perspective of my parents, too. No one wants to run out of money. If you live too long, you can run out of money. If you die too young, you never get to enjoy your money. Those are the two extremes of retirement.

Tammy and I talked about our parents, neither of whom got to enjoy a retirement. Running out of money will ruin your retirement, for sure. Having a lot of money will help you reach your goals of giving to charity or helping your children. But it doesn't do a thing for your hobbies or daily enjoyment of life.

I have clients who have millions of dollars, and all they do is watch FOX or CNN all day. They live in the most negative environments. I told my wife, we need to think about what we're going to do to have a successful retirement. My wife immediately went to money, but I said it's not the money that gives you a successful retirement. I told her, let's not be like our parents. So, we came up with some ideas we could love. Now, that's what I teach other people every day.

My wife and I came up with three critical categories and ruled out a fourth. Number one for us is travel. We are globetrotters. We go to Europe or do a big trip every year. We don't stay at the Ritz Carlton, but we also don't stay at the Motel 6. Between those worlds, we travel pretty well. We look for deals like everyone else, but we sit down and discuss where we want to go.

My wife knows I like setting things up, so she came up with a deal. She said, if I do all the work of booking flights and hotels and excursions, she will always be in a great mood and never complain if something got messed up, which happens on every trip. She said she didn't want to ever make me feel bad after doing all that work. She has stuck to it, because has never complained once. We go and try new things.

Last year, we took the family to Santa Barbara. We went to Florida to spend time with friends in Key West. We also took a trip to Tahiti, Bora Bora and Morea. Instead of going to Europe during COVID-19 shutdowns, we went to Alaska. I try to create trips of a lifetime, because travel is such a big thing. We do things a lot of people don't do, because travel is number one for us.

Number two is, we love great food. We make reservations at great restaurants, globally. But I also like to make great food at home. I have been studying how to be the best chef I can be. I think I'm a pretty good amateur chef right now. I'm working on my plating. My mother was a duly trained Julia Child chef in New York City, and she experimented on us all the time, which we loved. She had a saying: "If you give me your shoes and I cook them long enough in butter, they're going to be pretty tasty."

My wife and I made another agreement, where I do virtually all the cooking and most of the food shopping, and she does most of the cleaning up. However, she is the beneficiary of eating like we're in a five-star restaurant. If you eat a hamburger at my house, it's going to have layers of mushrooms, or sautéed spinach, or maybe even cashews.

Again, since I do this four or five nights out of seven, she told me she will never complain about it. Of course, I'm the biggest critic when it comes to taste. However, I enjoy being creative in the kitchen,and it's not always fancy. It can take me four hours to make an Italian sauce, because I want it to be just right. My meatloaf never tastes the same. If I was to start a TV cooking show, it would be called *The Leftover Man,* because I'm creative with whatever is in the fridge.

Our third criteria for enjoyment is red wine. We have studied and become sophisticated when it comes to red wine. I have more than a thousand bottles at home. I like big, bold, tannic or spicy red wines. Nothing wimpy. No Pinot. No Burgundy. I might have five bottles of those two and maybe five bottles of Chardonnay. The other 990 are bigger, bolder reds. We are constantly on the search for great wine. We love visiting wineries in Napa and Sonoma. My friends make fun of me, but we have become very discerning. We know what we like. And we even built a wine tasting room in our house, which is world class.

The fourth element is golf. We decided we like golf, rather than love golf, which allows us to lower our expectations of being good at it and enjoy it from where we are. My former business partner is an example of the opposite. He's a Type A obsessive personality and he took up golf. He decided in five years, if he doesn't shoot under an 80, he's going to quit. There may be one-percent of golfers who can shoot an 80. He said, "If you can't break an 85, you shouldn't even be playing." That would eliminate about 90-percent of all golfers.

He took lessons every week. He played three times a week. He went to the driving range. He lived on a golf course. He did everything a maniac does to be great at golf for five years. On the fifth anniversary of all his efforts, he went out and shot an 82. He put his clubs away and hasn't taken them out since. He was so obsessed with being great at golf, there was no opportunity to be good or enjoy it.

He forgot golf is also a social sport. The reason why so many deals are done on the golf course is not because we're competitive, it's because we're having a good time together. And when you have fun together, you break down barriers.

That's another reason why I prioritize fun at work. It's about breaking down barriers. You're having fun conversations about real life. Maybe you talk about a daughter who is disabled and the challenges you're going through. Or your divorce. Or sandwich generation challenges, where you have both a child and sick parents you're caring for. These things, and others like them, are real life situations most people go through in their lifetime.

The same is true for our clients. We don't take the arm's length approach that it's just about your money. We say, for example, tell me about you. My partner had much more of a rigid engineering style personality. He didn't want to know about people's personal lives. I brought in one of our largest clients, who was the COO of a large company. He was matter of fact and gravitated toward my partner's personality. I wanted to make sure I was still in the loop, because I brought him in.

We went out to lunch one day and he started talking about money. "Elliot, what do you think of the markets?" I responded, let me stop you for a second. I asked him if he had grandchildren? He said he did. I told him he never talks about his grandchildren. And then asked where they live and what he does with them. We had a whole conversation about his grandchildren, then about his wife. He didn't want to share any of his personal details originally, because he thought we were only about his money. That conversation changed the nature of our relationship completely.

When my son took his own life in 2015, that client was one of the first people who came into my office when I returned to work. He came in that day because he wanted to hug me. He sat down with me and he cried. He doesn't have suicide in his family. He cried, because he couldn't imagine that happening to him. That's making things human. We're not just automatons. We are humans. The human aspect means that what's important to you needs to be important to me. As a financial person, I think that's what it's all about. Some people call that listening skills. Whether it's your friends, your spouse, your child, or your client, if you don't know what's ticking inside of them, you won't keep them very long.

In my world, there are plenty of competent financial advisors. They work for lots of firms. Big firms, little firms, independent firms, and fiduciary firms like us. We are a boutique independent fiduciary firm. We're not the only good ones out there. There are lots of me's out there. I think what makes me unique is me. There are a lot of good firms out there, but there aren't as many people who want to know about you. I will talk about real life. You're in your second marriage? How's it going? Have you ever run into your ex? Yes, we did last week. How'd that go? You know what happened when I did that? My wife said... We can have a whole conversation about life.

Business is not just about the money. It's about life. It's about balancing all of what life throws at you. It's about understanding that balance is an illusion, but you need to do the best you can. Show up and create a life with as much balance as you can, when you can. And realizing each day is a new day to try. Find what makes you happy outside of work. Do anything you can to create a world for yourself, your family, friends, coworkers and employees that has a solid foundation in joy, respect and goals. Then shoot for them daily and if you miss, you have tomorrow. In business and life, you have to take the wins when you can.

PART THREE

YOU CAN DO IT

Chapter Thirteen

Your Brand Matters

– Adam Torres

"It takes 20 years to build a reputation and five minutes to ruin it. If you think about that, you'll do things differently."

~Warren Buffet

I'm sure you've heard the expression, "The riches are in the niches." It may sound counterintuitive, but the smaller your target audience, the greater your ability to dominate that audience. It's really about how you differentiate yourself and become an expert in a particular subject.

It's hard to be an expert in many different subjects. However, if you don't pick a particular area of expertise, you will spread yourself too thin and you won't be able to serve the clients you get as well as you should. If you're going in too many directions, you won't have time to improve your products, and you won't improve your delivery. When you concentrate on a single avatar you create content for, your message becomes crystal clear and focused. Without a niche, it's hard to plan. And, it's difficult to differentiate yourself from the competition.

When I prepare an interview for someone, and we're discussing what they should talk about, I put myself in the shoes of the audience. My goal is to create an interview when people watch it, they self identify with my interviewee, as someone they want to do business with.

For example, I did an interview with an accident lawyer in New York. He is a cyclist, and he works a lot of bicycle accident cases. I crafted the interview so if you were a bicycle rider in New York and you had been in an accident, you would want to call this lawyer. You would self identify, and know he's like me.

This lawyer is different from a general accident lawyer. When you listen to his interview, you hear how cycling became his passion and why he focuses on cyclists. His heart is in this niche. He gives various tips on how to stay safe, the rules of the road, your rights and what to do after an accident. He even shared his own accident story. If you're watching, as someone who needs a similar service, you are calling this one lawyer. You're not shopping around or checking his degree on the wall. You're in.

If you had a hyper-focused business, like being an accident attorney for cyclists, would you take a slip and fall case? Or would your next logical step be to open another firm focused on cyclists in another big city? Why only be the Bicycle Lawyer in New York? What are the top three cities in the country that have the most bicycles? You can scale your niche to be a huge business. As long as the thing you're focused on has enough of a market to achieve your goal, you're going to do well.

The way people think about how they attack a niche is what can be limiting. If you scale the bicycle lawyer idea, you can own that search term, and all of your marketing dollars are focused on that specific niche. You can go city by city to the point where if someone types the word "bicycle" into a search engine, the Bicycle Lawyer will show up at the top of the list. Period. Of course, it takes time to make it happen.

As an entrepreneur, if you're thinking you don't want to limit yourself to one niche, that is incorrect thinking. There is real power in focus. If you look at Mission Matters, we have built up a community of business owners, entrepreneurs and executives who are mission based. Do you know how many times people have told us we should be doing other things? But now, all these years later, we have a certain pedigree and clarity. That's how you build a brand.

The concept of a personal brand has changed over time. When I was growing up, the term personal brand was reserved for celebrities and athletes. When social media came about, most people didn't understand the power of it. People thought of it as signing up for another service. Slowly, society has begun to understand the concept of having a platform, and the importance and power of your voice being broadcast out to others.

Large companies have always understood this, because they have big budgets and hire professional teams who use television and radio for advertising. But, small businesses still lag behind on this understanding. Once a small business achieves some success with online platforms, things change. When a particular campaign brings in a certain amount of revenue and really moves the needle, things get serious. They no longer view social media as a Facebook Business Page or some online fad.

Advertising used to be the only game in town. But now, even if you do advertise, you need to back it up with some kind of content. You have to constantly be putting out content so people can see you or your company can actually deliver on your message and you are who you say you are as a person.

If you're the founder of a company, you matter now. Even if you're in a people-facing business development role, or if you're an up-and-coming manager who wants to move up the ranks in corporate America, if someone Googles your name, you need to be visible and you need to look good. If a potential client checks social media and they don't see any information to show who you are, or if none of it is professional, that's not going to support your journey.

If your competition is easily found and they have an appropriate professional presence that matches the role you are seeking, guess who's going to win? We are a smaller agency compared to some other media outlets, but we win business all the time that we wouldn't have gotten otherwise, due to our online presence. I've been on calls where the potential client says, "Adam, we were going to go with this other company, but I saw that interview you did and it spoke to me."

We are also not the least inexpensive company. People don't always choose the least expensive option. They go with who they trust, who they want to work with and who they think is going to bring them the most value. We've seen that over and over.

When I talk to business owners and tell them about the importance of creating content, I emphasize that they need to start now. You can't catch up over time. Even if you can't see an immediate ROI on the first day, you need to start. If you're putting yourself in a race and you're sitting at the starting line, while your competitor is moving ahead and producing content, you can't catch up in a day. If they have years of content, no amount of money can catch you up. You can't fake when something was posted or when an interview took place.

Individuals and business leaders who want to position themselves as thought leaders—because they actually are thought leaders and their voice should be heard—they should be out there promoting great ideas of their own, instead of the ideas of great marketers. There's a big difference between the two. In my opinion, there are still great ideas that are locked in the brains of the thought leaders who are not going public. That's where the real treasure trove is. That's why I try to help those thought leaders to get their message out there, because that's what's going to move our society forward.

I have nothing against the great marketers. They get a lot of good things out there. But this is one of the reasons why a lot of the messaging and the books we see are all the same. Those great marketers are out there marketing what sells. It's a self-fulfilling prophecy. There's a reason we're still talking about Jim Rohn and a host of other people, who have been teaching the same things forever. He got his inspiration from the Bible and it goes even further back. I'm a big Jim Rohn fan, but what I'm saying is the people who are out there innovating and changing the world, nobody knows about them, because they're not in the news. The big marketers are in the news all the time.

If you're an entrepreneur who struggles with shyness, or you think you're too old or too young, or too fat or too thin, or any other hang-up that would prevent you from putting yourself out there, you need to find the format that works for you and go with it. Not everyone should be doing video. Not everyone should be doing audio. I'm agnostic when it comes to what type of expression you want to use. When people ask me what type of content should I do, I tell them to do something. Do anything. Doing nothing will get you nowhere. If you've been doing nothing for many years, figure out what comes natural to you.

In the past, you had to train yourself to be a certain type of person for others to accept you as a thought leader in your space. You don't have to do that anymore. The only thing you have to do is be yourself and let other people have an opportunity to hear you, read you or do something with you.

Fear of presenting yourself online is not always what holds people back. It's a percentage, for sure. But some people don't see the importance of content. The number of people in business who still don't have websites is astounding. Everyone has an email, but you would be surprised how many people I meet, who tell me, "Oh, yeah, we've been meaning to get a website." Really? Go onto Wix or Squarespace and spend $50. Get a template. You need a website! Even if you have a corner store, Google might be how people find you.

Solving a marketing problem requires creative thinking. The most important thing you can do is to put yourself into the shoes of your client. How can you solve their problems? It's not about the ideas you come up with. It's about how you deliver them, and then what someone is willing to pay for them.

I'm not that creative. I'm not really an inventor of products, however, I am an inventor of models. I'm definitely an alchemist when it comes to meshing different models, types of distribution, and concepts in those areas. But my core products are not creative. Books, podcasts and marketing. I'm not inventing anything there. However, the ways we deliver those things are innovative.

In the past, when I was the interviewee, instead of the interviewer, I thought about what would have made various interviews a good experience for me. I think I waited a month before an interview was published. I then received some random email and, at that point, I had forgotten I was even on the show. Some shows don't even email you. And they're definitely not going to do any social media for you.

For my company, I was always looking at the experiences I had in the past that didn't work, in order to figure out how I could make them better. If we all looked at each of our similar situations a little deeper, it would move the needle. It doesn't mean you can do everything at once, but you can make a difference by being thoughtful about solving a problem, versus having to spend a bunch of money. Some of it may be rearranging schedules with the resources you already have.

By lengthening my interview times, when one interview ended, I had a little bit of free time to get some of the work done. That turned out to be much more effective than blocking off a full day to get all the editing done, and then releasing all the podcasts at once. It was basically an operational tweak.

In my mind, I was remembering the old Dominos' Pizza commercial that claimed you could have your pizza in 30 minutes or less. The commercial gave me the idea of getting a podcast out in 30 minutes or less. After I hired my first editor, we did achieve that goal. It's not our aim anymore, but with a team of editors, I could send them the recording as soon as I was done. They would have it edited and posted by the end of my next interview. And it wasn't one post. They created a whole marketing package and the podcast was posted everywhere 30 minutes after the interview.

Something as simple as speeding up content delivery had a huge effect on our brand. Everything you do affects your brand. Ultimately, your brand is who you are. I learned that from a very unlikely source: the billionaire founder of one of the largest mortgage brokers in the country.

My encounter with Dan Gilbert, the founder of Rock Financial and Quicken Loans, surprised and impressed me. When I first started working at Rock Financial, he was actually in my new hire class, giving part of the training. I still remember some of the things he used to say such as, "It's not who's right, it's what's right for the client."

In that class, Gilbert also told us a story about the importance of accountability that revealed the kind of person he is. The company had recently installed a new sign on the building. One of the mortgage bankers had worked late and when he left, he noticed one of the letters on the new sign was out. That meant all the people driving down the freeway were seeing a sign that looked bad. He called Gilbert directly to report this. At that point, I was thinking, why would he call the CEO about a sign? Gilbert took the call, contacted the sign company, and they shut it off until they could fix it.

Gilbert is all about accountability, and he was not above taking care of the sign. Then, he put his personal cell phone number on the whiteboard, and said, "If you have a problem, call me." Who does that? I've worked for a lot of companies and it doesn't happen. He was already successful, when he put his phone number on the whiteboard in front of a huge new hire class. That's what I call leading from the front.

He also did amazing things for his employees. He brought in Mark Cuban to talk to us in a private town hall meeting. He also brought in Kid Rock to perform for a Christmas party. He was way ahead of his time. Quicken Loans, which is now Rocket Mortgage, is a giant in the mortgage industry.

Gilbert set the tone for how I wanted to do leadership in my career. That was my first job out of college, and my first impression of an incredible leader. I had the luxury of being in that kind of environment and seeing his skills first-hand. I knew I wanted to grow into the same kind of a leader. The fact that I remember his teachings and his style of leadership so vividly, reveals the impression he made on me. It was a very big deal.

One of the main things I've implemented in my own business from my time at Quicken Loans is the idea that it's not about who's right, but what's right for the client. That way of thinking developed my thought process in business early on and it's a big deal for us at Mission Matters. It's how we position conversations in our organization.

There are so many ISMs, or systems, that got started at Quicken Loans. They have a whole book of them, including: "Obsessed with finding a better way," "Yes before No," "You'll see it when you believe it," "A penny saved is a penny."

One of my favorites I use all the time is: "We eat our own dog food." I'm not sure people know what it means, so I'll quote the book, *ISMs in Action,* by Dan Gilbert, directly, which says:

"Tying the threads and leveraging ideas and connections within our family of companies is what it's all about. That's what it means when we say we eat our own dog food. The basis of wealth is founded on the strength of relationships. Create them, seek them out, build upon them, be loyal to them. If your level of awareness is high, you will find an endless amount of dog food around you. The more you give to these relationships, the more you will get out of them. So, start giving now."

When I think about the way Mission Matters was built, it all started with a book. Then, the same group of clients asked us for podcasting help. We had already become experts in podcasting, because we produce our own shows. We leveraged those relationships. Then, we moved onto PR. That grew into having our own podcast network. We never really went outside of our network of people.

Even our employees have come from our business relationships. I met our Director of Marketing, because she was in one of our books. Even our co-founder, Chirag Sagar, who I met when I pitched for him to be in our first book. He thought it was a great idea, and said, "I want to work with you on the company." When I go down the line of everyone I do business with, I was probably introduced to them through an interview, they were in one of our books or we produced a show for them. We're all in the same ecosystem. That's what I mean by, we eat our own dog food.

When I think about why your brand matters, the first thing that comes to mind is creating a brand that is authentic to you and to your message. Authenticity makes you stand out when you're small, but it also scales. There are huge brands we all know, like Coca-Cola, because we grew up with them. And there are smaller, disruptive brands, like Nike once was, which have grown into huge brands, due to their authenticity. Nike broke through the mainstream barriers in 1980s athletic footwear by creating a marketplace based on their advertising and partnership with Michael Jordan. At the time, that was unheard of. However, the single shoe style launched in the 1980s, from a small company, is now one of the largest and most recognized brands in the world. The Jumpman division of Nike alone, with its unique logo and brand within a brand, is now bigger than most shoe companies as a whole.

It's easy to look at Nike's success and ask, how does it apply to me? I don't know if Michale Jordan had any idea how big the brand would become when he first signed the contract, but he made it what it became. He was always authentic around his brand, which allowed him to build trust with his audience over the course of decades. That trust is what creates an affinity with the Jumpman brand, in much the same way people have an affinity for Coca-Cola.

The lesson in this for small business owners is to be incredibly authentic around whatever brand you are creating. Be methodical about how you let people use it, how you use it and how you want it to be perceived. Remember, you are always building a brand, whether you realize it or not.

We do the same practices at Mission Matters when we put out content. We think about all the people who will be reading it. We think about all the content we have put out prior to a particular episode we may be working on. We are always thinking about if it's on brand or off brand. Does it make sense for our platform? Does it not make sense for our platform? If it doesn't make sense for our platform, we pass on it. We know we have the trust of our audience and that's something you can't get back once you lose it.

You don't have to go far to find your authenticity. It exists within you and around you. Theodore Roosevelt once said, "Do what you can with what you have." I've always used this principle in my life and my businesses. And what I've found is you probably have more than you need right in front of you. Possibly even more than you can handle if you focus on what's right in front of you. If you have one client, and if you focus on the one client and do a good job, it's likely you will get another client from the one you take care of. That's not necessarily why you do a good job, but it's a result of doing a good job. Most people stop a little short, because it doesn't happen immediately. However, if you keep at it, things usually blossom and you will get more from whatever you do. Be consistent. Deliver a good product. And hopefully, you have something people want. That's my philosophy of work and business dealings.

I feel like most people have an idea about what they want to do and they may overanalyze it to the point that it becomes an ordeal or frustration. Sometimes, you can do it and let it be the beta version or the minimum viable product.

I'll give you an example. I have a client right now who is a pretty big company. They sell a lot of purses and are a well-known brand, at least on the West Coast. They're looking at different marketing strategies for their luxury purse brand, and they asked me what I thought they should do.

After getting to know a little bit more about their business, I had a few ideas. I encouraged them to reach out and start creating relationships with other podcasters in the luxury market. They need to go after micro-influencers to help make their mark within that niche. They liked the strategy, but then asked me if I would do it for them. I told them that's not what we do. They replied, "But what if we're your first client and maybe it could become a new profit center for you?" That's what happens when you eat your own dog food. People want you to sign your name on a project, because they know you're going to come through for them.

The same can come from what's right in front of you. How did I meet a client? They were on my podcast. You can create new areas of business by being of service. It may not work for everyone, but you don't have to go outside of your niche or your vertical to add value to your brand. I stay in media as my niche, and can continue to expand my media platform. Our experience gives us the confidence to do that.

Chapter Fourteen

Confidence is Half the Battle

– Elliot Kallen

"Nurture your mind with great thoughts, for you will never go any higher than you think."

~Benjamin Disraeli

C onfidence is a belief in yourself. It's the conviction that you have the ability to meet life's challenges head on, and succeed. Confidence also gives you the willingness to act accordingly. Having a realistic sense of your own capabilities and feeling secure in your knowledge helps you project credibility, put others at ease and make a strong first impression.

The most important thing to understand about confidence is it's not a fixed characteristic. It's an ability you can acquire and improve over time. Setting and meeting goals can enable a belief in your own competence and capabilities. However, it requires a daily practice of facing and dealing with challenges, as well as getting help from the experts.

A long time ago, I participated in a Tony Robbins event called "Unleash the Power Within (or UPW)," where I had the opportunity to walk across hot coals with bare feet. It was a powerful exercise and I recommend it to everyone. Robbins works on the crowd for an entire day and you can feel there's some sort of hypnosis going on. It was after midnight when we all finally got up and walked outside to where the fire walk was taking place.

He asked us to buddy up with a person we didn't know, so I started talking to a woman who was in front of me in line. The fire was meant to represent a fear you were willing to overcome.

The woman in front of me was from Boston. She was in the process of moving up the corporate ladder and she was afraid she would end up leaving all her friends behind. She was afraid of sabotaging her own success for friendships, and felt she would be compromising her soul to sabotage herself. We had a long talk about friendships and solidified real friends don't do that to each other, unless one of them becomes a snob.

Then, she asked me what my fear was. At that time, I told her I either want to be in the front of the pack, at the back or not participating. My fear was being in the middle. I didn't want to be the nondescript, non-entity, not winning and not losing, merely participating in the race type of person. Only participating in life. We all participate in some things, but I wanted to be the person who excels. I wanted to know when to excel and when to walk away, because the middle road is not for me.

We talked about my fears and I told her about my dad. He worked a hundred hours a week and he never got to enjoy his retirement. To me, that's a person who never really enjoyed life. He didn't live life to the fullest. Did he have enjoyable moments? Yes. He had a good marriage with my mother and he had good moments with his children. Maybe a couple of good vacations. But he was mostly consumed with trying to make a living. I didn't want to be that person. My fire walk helped me focus on creating a life vision, not necessarily a business vision. And I still live by that vision today.

Excelling at something gives you confidence. If you want to become good at something, become an expert at it. It takes study. Some things you can learn quickly, while other things take years to learn. About 20 years ago, I decided

I wanted to be an expert on California wines. So, I decided to go out and try everything to learn what I liked.

What I discovered early in that process was everything I didn't like. It worked exactly opposite of what I thought would happen. Obviously, I kept at it long enough to discover what I did like, which is big, strong, bold red wines. No wimpy red wines for me. Those bold wines match my personality. I am strong, wide, approachable, but not soft and delicate. I am not a Pinot.

I learned that with white wines, I don't like the taste of oak. With reds, I don't like grassy or earthy tastes. Becoming an expert is often about finding out what you don't like. I tell my kids that dating is not about finding the right person. It's about ruling out all the wrong people. The same thing is true for business. It's about ruling out what won't work, which rules in what may work. The attainable may be far more appealing than the unrealistic.

My wife is much prettier than me and way nicer, too. She's from the upper peninsula of Michigan and I'm from New Jersey, which I consider the crude side of the world. We all think we're Tony Soprano from the hit HBO series *The Sopranos*, because we're from New Jersey. When we first started dating, we took a Friday off of work and drove up to David Coffaro Winery in Healdsburg, in Sonoma County. I warned her it was my fourth time going there.

The first time, a date took me there. I liked the guy who ran the winery and I wanted to impress my date, so I bought a case of wine that would be ready about 18 months later. After we broke up, I got a postcard in the mail to come pick up my wine. So, I took another date there. We picked up the wine and broke up right after. Then, I took another date there and we broke up on the way home from the winery. I asked Tammy, "Are you sure you're comfortable going there?" She said she would take her chances. I also informed her I was still doing research, trying to find out what wine I liked. I couldn't narrow it down.

When we got there, the owner, David, was pouring the wine, which is unusual. He was in his 60s and cantankerous. He was a bit of a hippie, who made his money in early technology, then left to open a winery. As he was pouring, I asked if he remembered me. He said, "I don't know your name, but I know I've seen you at a few of our events." I responded, "I come here every year, to this bottle tasting. I buy wine and I never drink it at home. I want you to know I really like some of your red wine. And some of it has been awful."

Tammy was looking at me like, you're really saying this to this guy? But he took it really well. Then he said, "I have 18 barrels of red wine here we can sample. Why don't we sample them and see what you do like." I thought, wow, what a generous offer. He didn't even charge me. He did it out of the kindness of his heart. He said, "You two are the only people who have been in here all day, so let's do it."

The first barrel happened to be an Italian varietal. David takes the long thing that looks like a bovine impregnator, siphons up some wine and puts it into glasses for us. We all took a sip and I said, "That sucks." Tammy looked at me like, that was so rude! I looked at David and said, "I'm so sorry. That was rude." He responded, "You taught me something about your taste. We're going to eliminate six other barrels here, because if you don't like this one, you won't like those either."

When we finished sampling the whole barrel room, I told him my favorite was the Block 4 and my second favorite was his Zinfandel. He was a red zin house. That was interesting, because all I have at home is the Block 4. Then I asked him, "David, you've been dealing with people for 20 years. What did you learn about me, other than I can be a real jerk?" He responded, "Ninety-percent of Americans, maybe more, have the same relative number of taste buds on their tongues. They taste a little bit of everything on their tongues. Salt is good. Sugar is good. Mexican food is good, hot stuff, not so good. You are not in that 90-percent. Five-percent of Americans have a lot more than the average number of taste buds. They can taste the soft Pinot velvet. They can tell the different areas of Italy in the wine. They are really discerning drinkers. You're not one of those, either. You are in the five-percent who have too few taste buds and you need bigger, bolder, spicier, tannic wine to be able to enjoy it."

He asked me if I liked spicy food and blackened fish. I said, yes, I love blackened fish. He said it was due to the fact that they have more spices on them. He asked me what spices I overuse in the kitchen and I told him garlic. It turned out, I needed more garlic to taste it. The same was true with my red wine choices. I learned something new about my palate. We ended up joining new wine clubs, canceling old wine clubs and buying wine that was bigger and suddenly, wine became an avocation of ours. It's a fun thing Tammy and I do together.

Tammy bought me a beautiful, full-sized wine fridge that was embellished with red mahogany. The four cases of wine I had been storing in a closet were transferred into it immediately. It holds about 191 bottles and we filled it up pretty quickly. We built a beautiful wine room on the other side of the garage and now, we have wine parties. We have 1,000 bottles of wine filling slots and about eight cases waiting to be unpacked, which is over the top. We need to have more wine parties. We took a hobby and treated it like a business. We learned what we love about buying and drinking wine, and it became fun.

I get a lot of complaints about my wine collection. I don't have enough varietals. I have spicy Zins, big tannic cabs, a Meritage, but not a Bordeaux, not a Pinot, not a Burgundy, and no Italian varietals. People are critical of that. It's the same in business. People say you keep doing these two or three things, and what about this other thing? I don't need to do that, because what I'm currently doing is working really well. If it's not working well, you may need to diversify.

Some people say I'm overly discerning. But I want to figure out what works. So many business owners learn what works, then they try the exact opposite. They start playing to their weaknesses, rather than their strengths. Successful companies always play to their strengths and deal with their weaknesses. But entrepreneurs are always trying new things that don't work or unwittingly stopping things that do work. This is how they self-destruct.

I see people, especially in my industry, doing this. Let's say direct mail and seminars are working for you. But you haven't been doing any dinners, and those seem to be working for your competitors. So, you stop doing seminars that were making you money, and spend a bunch of money to now do dinners. Then you wonder why it's not working.

Companies that really knock it out of the park tend to do one, two or three things extremely well, and they do it over and over. They are experts. That's what you want to do. Focus on your core competency and do it better than anyone else. You will have more confidence than you ever imagined.

Chapter Fifteen

Impact Your World

– Elliot Kallen

"We exist temporarily through what we take, but we live forever through what we give."

~Vernon Jordan

What does it mean to have an impact on the world? In recent years, this expression has become so ubiquitous, it's become almost cliché. People want to work for companies that have a reputation for positively impacting the world. But a lot of that gets lost in marketing speak and we tend to forget our neighbor could use some help. It's not exactly easy to impact **the** world. But you can absolutely impact **your** world.

A definition of impact that makes it personal and real comes from Sir Ronald Cohen's latest book, *On Impact: The Guide to the Impact Revolution*. He defines impact in this way: "An impact is the measure of an action's benefit to society and the planet." In other words, every action you take can be looked at in terms of how it affects people and the planet.

Making an impact involves doing your part to contribute to a better future for yourself, your family, your community and your environment. Charity begins right where you are.

When I was young, I wanted to be a doctor. Unfortunately, my science teachers were yo-yos and they turned me off of science. When I was in fourth grade, Dr. DeBakey did one of the first heart transplants in the world and it was filmed and shown on a PBS television special. My mother made us watch it and at nine years old, I decided I wanted to be a heart surgeon.

When I heard they were going to do a heart transplant in New York, I wrote a letter in my own handwriting to Dr. Adrian Kantrowitz, who was at Maimonides Hospital, in Brooklyn, telling him I wanted to be a heart surgeon and asked if he would help me. My mother mailed it and she received a call from his secretary, saying he would love to help. He offered to let me spend the day with him in surgery and doing rounds, with my own personalized lab coat. My mother set it up so my brother would come with me. We took a Friday off school and went to the hospital, where we received our personalized lab coats. He gave my letter back to me with a personal note, which I still have.

We went on rounds, visiting patients. Then, he said, "We're going to do a heart transplant downstairs, between two German Shepherds. Would you like to be involved with this?" We were like, "Wow! That's cool!" My older brother said we could do it, but he didn't want me to see the first cut, because it would be too scary. After the first cut, they let me in. I had on gloves and a mask, and the doctor asked me if I wanted to hold the rib spreader. I did it. Then, he asked if I wanted to hold the dog's lungs open, while they removed the heart. I did it briefly, then the adults took over. They had the first heart-lung machine in the U.S., so they could keep the dog alive without a heart. My brother was in the other room with the other dog, doing the same thing. That actually happened, and it was a huge life lesson.

My dad was so proud of me, but in time, it became annoying. He took me with him everywhere and had me tell the story of the heart transplant. I went to the school library and read every book they had on the human heart. I came up with a two-minute version of how the heart works. I must have told that story 300 times to all of his clients as his nine, 10, and 11-year-old sales manager. He would kvell, which is a great Yiddish word that means to be extraordinarily proud. His chest would swell, as he said, "My son, the future doctor." Unfortunately, in eighth and ninth grade, I had terrible science teachers who turned me off of science.

The biggest lesson I learned from the experience was you can do anything and be anything you want. Most limits are self-imposed. They're not as real as we think. And that's true in entrepreneurship, too. There are some people who break free of those limits. Whether you love him or hate him, Elon Musk has certainly demonstrated how to break free of limits. As has Jeff Bezos, as well as many others. They understand there are no limits. Sometimes, they end up with their foot in their mouth, but that's another issue.

A different kind of limit involves our self-destructive side. We can feel unworthy of success. When we feel that way in business or our marriage, we start acting in self-destructive ways.

A lot of people are either running toward something in life, or running away from something. We do the same thing in business. We are either running toward success, or running away from failure.

Let me speak from a male point of view for just a second. I think too many men are running away from their marriage and their children. I don't mean by going to the bar and getting drunk. That's a different issue. But they are filling up their time when they should be with family, a spouse or even business time.

My son-in-law is going to the gym twice a day and his wife is pregnant. I asked my daughter what was going to happen when they had a kid. She said, "We're going to put a gym in the house." I told her the time when he's working out for an hour and a half twice a day, is time he's not with the kids. And you are. That's not a good recipe for family success.

My father-in-law was a project guy. He decided to redo the bathroom. It took five months. He worked on it every Saturday and Sunday. You know what else was happening on Saturday and Sunday? Soccer, football and baseball for his kids. But he couldn't go, because he was fixing the bathroom or working on his car. He was getting out of things.

A friend of mine bought a boat when his kids were young. He worked on the boat every weekend, so he wouldn't have to go to his kids' sporting events. He would say he was working on the boat so it would be safe for them when they came on it. He didn't go to one soccer game and he's proud of it. I think we, as humans, tend to fill up our lives with stuff.

In business, if you have something you have to do from nine to 11 every day and you hate it, you will find something else to do. I'm guilty of it, too. I meet with vendors in my business, then go for an extended lunch, instead of getting on LinkedIn and doing what I need to do. Mostly, because LinkedIn is unpleasant for me. As humans, sometimes we run away from what's important and run toward something that's unimportant, but timely.

I've seen a graph with four quadrants, where the top left quadrant is labeled **Urgent** and Important. The top right quadrant is **Not Urgent, but Important**. Bottom left is **Urgent, but Not Important** and the bottom right is **Not Urgent and Not Important**. The vertical axis shows importance. The higher you go, the more important. The horizontal axis shows urgency. To the left is **Urgent**, and to the right is **Not Urgent**.

You can categorize what you need to do into these four quadrants to prioritize your daily activities. Focus on the **Urgent and Important** things first. Do these right away. If it's **Important, but Not Urgent**, these tasks need to be scheduled. Plan to do them as soon as you can. If it's **Urgent, but Not Important**, delegate those tasks so they don't eat up large portions of your day. And if it's **Not Urgent and Not Important**, get rid of it or postpone it. We often use these tasks as an excuse to escape the drudgery of other tasks. Don't let procrastination derail you from success.

When you look at everything you do in a day, and put all those tasks into the appropriate quadrants, it's amazing how many things end up in the **Not Urgent and Not Important** quadrant. Also, it's surprising how few things we accomplish every day of the week were actually **Important** in one of the listed ways. Imagine how much more efficient we would be if we tackled the **Important** things first, every day. Then move onto the other boxes and leave the **Not Urgent and Not Important** things for one Saturday a month.

Men who are creating projects to run away from their families have made the bathroom remodel **Important**. My dad was not a project guy. He was not good with a hammer, at all. When I got my first house and started doing projects, he said to me, "Elliot, you have to decide what kind of a person you want to be. If you're going to be a project guy, that's great. You'll save lots of money doing it yourself. But the cost will be the time you could have spent at work, improving yourself or being a good husband and a great father." It's a choice. You can be a project guy, or you can pay more to hire it out and have more time to do what is **Important**.

One of the ways my wife makes fun of me is when she doesn't expect me to be able to fix anything. She's going to hire someone instead. Every once in a while, I get out my tools and start to fix something, and she says she's shocked. I told her she embarrassed me and I have to do it now. She responds to me saying I should hire someone, because she'd rather go for a hike. "Just because I made fun of you, doesn't necessarily mean I want you to change as much as I want to make fun of you." And because of my sense of humor, I'm okay with it and we go for a hike.

Both your business life and your personal life can be prioritized in this way. If you want to impact your world, do what's **Important** now, and put everything else on the back burner. Whatever falls into those other three quadrants, you can probably hire people to help you with. Painting my bedroom is not the most important thing I do this weekend. Getting it painted might be, but painting it myself is not. There's a profound difference.

You can do anything you decide you want to do. You can impact your little corner of the world, or the entire globe. All you have to do is choose to be the person who does it.

Conclusion

The reason we chose the word *Driven* for the title of this book, is because you cannot be successful without an amazing drive to reach your goals. You don't need to have every goal defined. The road you travel will help you define your goals, and sometimes define you. But if you're waking up and not thinking about what you have to do, and how you're going to do it, you probably shouldn't be an entrepreneur. You may be better suited to working for someone else. And there's nothing wrong with that. In fact, the same drive will make you a success in the corporate world, too.

The top entrepreneurs in every industry have amazing drive. They wake up wanting to accomplish their goals or bring their message to the market. Their market can be a for-profit business or a nonprofit. It can even be religious. But you want to bring your message home all the time.

Being driven is part of what it takes to build a strong character, one who doesn't give up. The path of the entrepreneur is never a smooth one, that's for sure. Things happen and you will have to zig and zag. Being driven equates to being relentless—never giving up. That's what it takes to run your own business.

If you take anything from this book, we hope it's a focus on the journey, rather than the result. There are a few people out there who have a straight line to success, or so it appears from the outside. But more often than not, you will encounter roadblocks and obstacles. Roadblocks and obstacles are merely that. They are not cliffs. And they are not stop signs. They are obstacles. Those obstacles could be things like running out of money, serious health problems, a death in the family, divorce, a business failure, credit problems or accounts receivable issues. If you face your challenges head-on and deal with them one at a time, you can create a stronger result than if you let those challenges run you over. And if you don't face them head-on, they will run you over at some point.

Let perseverance be the driver that keeps you on your road to success, and let character allow you to achieve your goals without having to leave your family, your friends and all the things that matter to you behind.

We hope our stories spark ideas that catalyze you to move forward in your business ventures, or inspire you to step out and do something you've always dreamed of doing. Our intention around sharing our entrepreneurial journeys is to help you avoid the most common mistakes, and to help you understand what it means to be an entrepreneur.

Most of all, we want our stories to inspire you to know, if we can do this, you can, too.

If this book has inspired you, please share it with your friends. Whether that's in the form of a conversation or a social media post about a concept you learned, the best way to hold onto inspiration and to gain momentum is to share your new information with others. The more we share, the more information we retain, and the more we are inspired to action.

We wish you great success in your business and your life.

— Adam Torres and Elliot Kallen

AN INVITATION FROM ADAM TORRES

I hope you enjoyed this book and that it brings you
the inspiration you need to create your own
version of work, success and happiness!
If you'd like to connect with me,
please connect here:

You can also connect with me on Facebook,
Instagram, YouTube, Etc.
For additional books,
visit and follow my Amazon page:
(https://www.amazon.com/
stores/author/B01MZ6GIJ0)
Also, check out my podcast,
Mission Matters at www.MissionMatters.com

AN INVITATION FROM ELLIOT KALLEN

Having a fulfilling life as an entrepreneur is tough,
but I hope this book gives you inspiration
and ideas to turbo-charge your path to success.

If you'd like to connect with me,
please visit my website,
Prosperity Financial Group
(www.prosperityfinancialgroup.com)

Also, check out my podcast, Meet The Expert with Elliot Kallen
(https://prosperityfinancialgroup.com/
meet-the-investing-expert-with-elliot-kallen/)

If you would like to learn more about A Brighter Day
nonprofit, visit our website (ABrighterDay.info)

APPENDIX

ABOUT A BRIGHTER DAY CHARITY

Nestled in San Ramon, Calif., A Brighter Day stands as a beacon of hope for teen mental wellbeing and suicide prevention. Born in 2015, with a fervent aspiration to stop teen suicides, the 501(c)(3) charity has evolved to champion parental support and education. The team is passionately committed to mental health awareness, targeting adolescents and their guardians with resources, engaging events and digital insights. Bound by the goal of reshaping the narrative around teen mental health, the charity is driven by the belief that every individual, teen and parent deserves brighter days.

Core Programs

- *Crisis Text Line:* An immediate support line for anyone in crisis. Available 24/7, it connects individuals with trained crisis counselors who can provide support in times of need. Text BRIGHTER to 741741.

- *Teletherapy:* Recognizing the growing need for remote support, the virtual therapy program allows teens and families to connect with trained therapists from the comfort of their homes. Vouchers are available for those in financial need.

- *Article Center:* A comprehensive hub of articles, insights and guidance that addresses the varied aspects of teen mental health, offering solace and solutions.

- *Parent and Teen Resource Kit:* Designed to equip both teens and their guardians with knowledge, the kits are filled with informative materials, tips and tools to navigate the challenging terrains of adolescence.

Ways to Support

Apart from seeking help, individuals might be interested in supporting the cause. Here's how to make a difference:

- *Donate:* Financial support can help A Brighter Day continue its mission. Visit the website to contribute.

- *Volunteer:* Join the team and be a part of the change. Whether it's by facilitating events, offering teletherapy or creating content, your skills are valuable. Reach out to get started.

- *Spread Awareness:* Become an ambassador for mental wellbeing. Share our resources, talk about teen mental health, and help us break the stigma. Every conversation can make a difference.

Get in Touch

To access resources, seek support, or get involved, contact us:

Website: www.abrighterday.org

Email: support@abrighterday.info or elliot@abrighterday.info

Phone: (510) 206-1103

Address: 411 Read Dr., Lafayette, CA 94549

Recommended Reading

While our resources aim to provide comprehensive guidance, we also understand the value of continual learning. We recommend the following for further insights into teen mental health: *Supporting Student Mental Health: Essentials for Teachers,* by Michael Hass and Amy Ardell.

This book offers invaluable insights for educators and individuals alike. Recognizing that teachers play a pivotal role not just in academic instruction, but also in socio-emotional support, it provides actionable strategies to address students' mental health needs. Get your copy on Amazon at https://a.co/d/4S7kp8v

Uniting Depression and Stress Resources with Teenagers

Made in the USA
Columbia, SC
20 November 2023